TENSE SITUATIONS

TENSE SITUATIONS

Tenses in Contrast and Context

Pamela Hartmann
Annette Zarian
Patricia Esparza

THOMSON
~TM
HEINLE

Australia Canada Mexico Singapore Spain United Kingdom United States

THOMSON

★ ™

HEINLE

Tense Situations
Tenses in Contrast and Context
Hartman • Zarian • Esparza

Associate Publisher: *Chris Carson*
Acquisitions Editor: *Susan Marshall*
Production Manager: *Debra A. Jenkin*
Manufacturing Manager: *Kimberly Powell*
Development and Production: *M. E. Aslett Corporation*

Printed in the United States of America
   6 7 8 9 10   06 05 04 03 02

For more information contact Heinle, 25 Thomson Place, Boston, MA 02210 USA,
or you can visit our Internet site at http://www.heinle.com

ISBN: 0-03-022517-5

Library of Congress Catalog Card Number:

TEACHER'S NOTES

Tense Situations is intended for high-intermediate ESL students who have studied all or most of the tenses in English but haven't mastered them completely. Such students may have difficulty "juggling" several tenses at once because they have studied each tense in isolation or, at best, in contrast with only one other tense. In addition, they may not have studied any tense within a complete context. It's important for students at this stage to learn to integrate the various tenses and to understand the shades of meaning of each tense; *Tense Situations* guides students toward this end by focusing on tenses **in contrast with** and **in the context of** complete stories. Frequent review and recycling prevents students from forgetting one tense as they learn a new one.

This text can be useful as either a self-study book or a classroom textbook for students who know about the various tenses but don't use them in free conversation or writing. Instead, these students tend to fixate on just a few select tenses: the **simple present** ("I write a letter right now."), **simple past** ("I drove down the freeway when I saw an accident."), and **simple future** with "will" ("I will watch TV tonight."). Their use of the language is stilted, unnatural, and often ungrammatical because of their inability to utilize the complete range of tenses.

Tense Situations can also be used as a reference by teachers and students alike. Rules for the use of each tense are found within the chapters; in addition, the appendix offers a series of charts on the use of tenses in subordinate clauses, indirect speech, the passive voice, and the basic conditional.

The book was not intended to encompass all facets of verb usage. Modals, the conditional, the passive voice, and indirect speech have not been included, except in the appendix, so that attention may be focused on a thorough treatment of the tenses themselves. One chapter, for example, is devoted to the difference between "will" and "be going to"; this difference is often ignored in ESL classrooms but needs to be mastered if the student is to avoid awkward, unnatural, or misleading language.

The artwork used throughout the text is, for the most part, functional. An attempt has been made to portray the abstract notions of time and tense as concretely—as visually—as possible. The careful arrangement of pictures within the frames in the filmstrip stories allows students to visualize the relationship of one tense to another; wherever possible, "before now" or "before then" is to the left, and "after now" or "after then" is to the right, corresponding to the notion of the time lines on which "past" is to the left and "future" is to the right. For example, in the filmstrip story depicting future perfect, the narrator ("now") is placed in the far left corner of the frame and the "future" action on the far right. The "future perfect" action is placed in a bubble to the left of the "future," signifying its placement in time—that is, before another future action.

The authors hope that the use of humorous—sometimes outrageous—characters and situations will make this sometimes insufferable subject not only sufferable but, perhaps, even enjoyable!

Use of the Book

All chapters except for the review chapters should be presented using the following steps:

1. Students read the filmstrip story on the left of the page. The teacher may introduce new vocabulary before students begin to read the filmstrip story or may check their understanding of it afterwards. Most new vocabulary items have been recycled elsewhere in the text.

2. Students then go back to the beginning, cover up the story on the left, and read the story on the right; this time they choose the correct tense for each simple verb form.

3. Students read the explanations. (Depending on the students' level, steps 1 and 2 may be done in reverse order.) Whenever possible, the explanations contain examples taken from the filmstrip stories. Because space limitations have restricted the number of examples that could be included, teachers may want to point out additional examples from the filmstrip story or from their students' lives.

4. The teacher guides students through the directions and examples for the "Rap It Up" section (oral exercises). Then students work in pairs independently of the teacher.

5. For the "Fill It In" section or the "Picture Puzzle" (alternate chapters), the teacher guides students through the first few sentences. The picture puzzles will probably require additional explanation, at least initially. One successful method is for the teacher to put many of the picture puzzle symbols and one sample sentence on the board, silently point to each, and have the class guess the meanings before actually beginning to write. The students soon learn the common symbols and have little need for the "Key to Symbols" at the back of the book.

6. "Rap in the Real World" is intended to allow students to apply what they've learned to their own lives.

For the review chapters:

1. Students fill in the blanks in the story.

2. Students rewrite the story—without looking back at it—with the aid of the "Cue Sheet."

3. Using the information on the "Story Line," students answer the questions on the page following. This may be done orally or in writing, depending on the level and focus of the class.

4. Students practice the targeted tenses in role play or discussion related to their own lives.

For the cumulative review chapters:

1. Students fill in the blanks in the story. Because these stories are quite long, they have been divided into sections. Students might do section 1 in class, section 2 for homework, and section 3 in class the next day. The teacher should encourage the class to keep in mind the entire context instead of concentrating on each sentence as a separate entity.

2. Students work in pairs or groups on the "Rap It Up" section.

ANSWER KEYS

For the sake of style and the use of natural language, contractions have been used wherever possible. Where several tenses are possible in a given situation, these have been indicated. The teacher may refer students to explanation pages or reference charts if there is any confusion. It may sometimes be frustrating to find multiple possibilities; however, this is the nature of the language, and to present exercises without such complexity would mean creating unnatural linguistic situations.

ACKNOWLEDGMENTS

The authors would like to thank Jean Zukowski/Faust and Anne Boynton-Trigg of Holt, Rinehart and Winston; Yves Jacot for the initial inspiration; our patient reviewers (Lida Baker, of UCLA; Gloria Brambilla, of the Los Angeles Unified School District; and Judy Gough, of Santa Monica College); Ann Snow of UCLA, for help with the Appendix; and Don Robb, for uncomplainingly squeezing casts of thousands into incredibly small spaces. For help on the second edition, many thanks go to editor Susan Marshall, the wonderful production people at M. E. Aslett Corporation, and Mike Linden-Martin for his diligent review.

CONTENTS

PRESENT

PAST

FUTURE

APPENDIX

TENSE SITUATIONS

PRESENT

1 Present Continuous
Simple Present

2 Present Perfect
Simple Present

3 Present Perfect Continuous
Present Continuous

4 Present Tense Review

Read the story on the left. When you finish, go back to the beginning, cover up the story on the left, and choose the correct tense for each capitalized simple form of the verb to the right of the picture.

THE HOLIDAY CRUISE

My name is James Sterling. I'm the cruise director on the *Holiday Princess*. Every week our ship *sails* around the Caribbean full of passengers.

The people on the ship *are* always *looking* for fun and excitement. Let's look at some of the people on board this week.

Here *is* Mr. Rodney Tyler. He *is* a very charming man. He *is enjoying* this trip very much right now.

At this moment he *is sitting* in the middle of a group of women.

My name is James Sterling. I'm the cruise director on the *Holiday Princess*. Every week our ship SAIL around the Caribbean full of passengers.

The people on the ship always LOOK for fun and excitement. Let's look at some of the people on board this week.

Here BE Mr. Rodney Tyler. He BE a very charming man. He ENJOY this trip very much right now.

At this moment he SIT in the middle of a group of women.

He is *entertaining* them with funny stories, *offering* them champagne, and *laughing* at their jokes. In fact, he *seems* to be the life of the party.

In his everyday life, however, Rodney Tyler *is* a very shy man.

He *is working* temporarily as a computer programmer. At work, he *sits* by himself in front of his computer screen.

He rarely *looks* at people and usually *spends* his time daydreaming.

And there *is* Mr. Horace Pennington III. He *is relaxing* this week.

Look! He *is lying* in his chair and *reading* a novel. And *isn't* there music *coming* from the radio beside him?

He ENTERTAIN them with funny stories, OFFER them champagne, and LAUGH at their jokes. In fact, he SEEM to be the life of the party.

In his everyday life, however, Rodney Tyler BE a very shy man.

He WORK temporarily as a computer programmer. At work, he SIT by himself in front of his computer screen.

He rarely LOOK at people and usually SPEND his time daydreaming.

And there BE Mr. Horace Pennington III. He RELAX this week.

Look! He LIE in his chair and READ a novel. And NOT BE there music COME from the radio beside him?

At home, by contrast, Horace Pennington never *relaxes*.

He hardly ever *reads* novels; instead, every morning he *reads* the business news in the *Wall Street Journal*. . .

. . . and *listens* to the news of the stock market on his car radio as he *goes* to work.

Why, I *don't believe* my eyes. *Is* that Ellen Wiggley?

Look, she's *jogging* around the ship!

My gosh, now she's even *doing* jumping jacks!

At home, by contrast, Horace Pennington never RELAX.

He hardly ever READ novels; instead, every morning he READ the business news in the *Wall Street Journal*. . .

. . . and LISTEN to the news of the stock market on his car radio as he GO to work.

Why, I NOT BELIEVE my eyes. BE that Ellen Wiggley?

Look, she JOG around the ship!

My gosh, now she even DO jumping jacks!

This is amazing! When Ellen is at home, she's a real couch potato. She's always *complaining* that she *wants* to exercise, but somehow she rarely *does* more than watch TV.

Now the ship *is coming* back to port. The passengers *are thinking* about changing their everyday lives. Rodney *hopes* always to enjoy life as he *is enjoying* it at this moment.

Horace *is promising* himself to relax as he *is relaxing* at present.

And Ellen *wants* to exercise as she *is doing* right now.

Ah. Here they all are now. They*'re leaving* the ship and *throwing* their promises overboard.

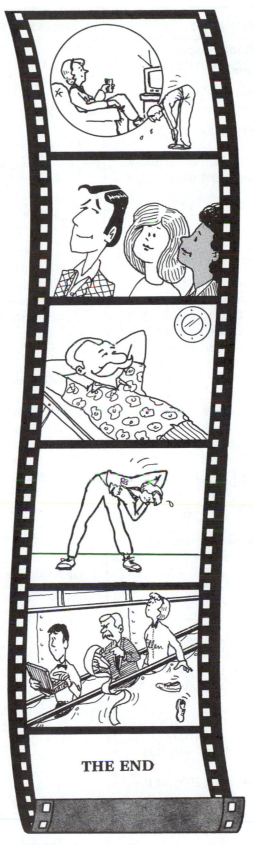

THE END

This is amazing! When Ellen is at home, she BE a real couch potato. She always COMPLAIN that she WANT to exercise, but somehow she rarely DO more than watch TV.

Now the ship COME back to port. The passengers THINK about changing their everyday lives. Rodney HOPE always to enjoy life as he ENJOY it at this moment.

Horace PROMISE himself to relax as he RELAX at present.

And Ellen WANT to exercise as she DO right now.

Ah. Here they all are now. They LEAVE the ship and THROW their promises overboard.

PRESENT CONTINUOUS	SIMPLE PRESENT

1. The **present continuous** expresses an action that is happening right now.
 	
———————|———————
                        NOW
 	
They*'re leaving* the ship.
 	
NON-ACTION verbs do not usually occur in the **present continuous**. (See pages 9–11.)
	The **simple present** is used with a NON-ACTION verb to indicate something that is happening right now.
	
	———————|———————
	                        NOW
	
	She *seems* happy.
	This *tastes* good.
	I don't *believe* my eyes!
	
	See pages 9–11 for a list of these verbs.

2. The **present continuous** also expresses an action (repeated, or of long duration) in a time period that *includes* the present moment. However, the action is not necessarily happening right now. The **present continuous** is used in this way for a *temporary* activity.
 	
—————×—×—×—×|×—×————
                        NOW
 	
Rodney Tyler *is working* temporarily as a computer programmer.
 	
———————|———————
                        NOW
 	
Horace Pennington *is relaxing* this week.
	The **simple present** expresses:
	a. an action that is repeated habitually (for example: often, sometimes, every day, once a week);
	
	—————×—×—×—×|×—×————
	                        NOW
	
	He *reads* the business news every morning.
	
	b. a general truth that is repeated periodically;
	
	The sun *sets* in the west.
	
	c. a condition that is not repeated but is always true.
	
	———————|———————
	                        NOW
	
	Ellen Wiggley *loves* chocolate.

3. The **present continuous** is used for a very frequent activity about which we feel some emotion. We use it with the adverbs *always*, *forever*, or *constantly*. ————×—×—×—×—×—×|×—×—×—— NOW She*'s* always *complaining*. (irritation) The adverb comes between BE and the present participle.	

	PRESENT CONTINUOUS	SIMPLE PRESENT
4.	We often use the **present continuous** after the word *while*. *While* indicates a continuous action at the same time as another action. There are two possible positions in the sentence for a clause beginning with *while*. While his brothers *are helping* the passengers on the boat, Mark just sits there and does nothing. (comma) Mark just sits there and does nothing while his brothers *are helping* the passengers. (no comma)	When the **simple present** is used after *while*, it indicates a continuous action. She *tries* to look like a normal shopper while she *does* her job catching shoplifters. (For more on *while*, see Chapters 6 and 15.)
5.	When we have a compound verb, the verb BE is omitted from the second action. He *is lying* in his deck chair and *reading* a novel.	

6.	We often use the **present continuous** with these words:
	
	see box #1 (right) now
	                   at the (this) moment
	                   at present
	
	see box #2 these days, nowadays
	                   today
	                   this week, month, year
	                   this semester, quarter, and so on
	
	see box #3 always
	                   forever
	                   constantly
		We often use the **simple present** with these words:
		
		always
		often
		frequently
		usually
		sometimes
		every day, week, month, and so on
		once a week, month, year, and so on
		occasionally
		seldom
		rarely
		never

7.		In casual conversation, especially in lengthy narration, the **simple present** can refer to past events. "So she *runs* into the room and *screams* that there's a UFO on the lawn."

For additional uses of the **present continuous** and **simple present**, see Chapters 14 and 15.

Rap It Up

Oral Practice: Work with one other student. Make up as many sentences as you can about the following pictures. Use the **present continuous** and **simple present** tenses. Use the vocabulary words under the pictures.

The *Nile Queen* is now sailing down the Nile River. Here are three passengers. What are they doing now, and what do they usually do at home?

Examples: She is swimming (now/at this moment/and so on).
She (usually/often/sometimes/and so on) watches TV.

On the cruise   At home

dance*

listen to music

swim*

Grandmother

watch TV

knit

use a computer

drown

play tennis

fish*

Policeman

chase robbers

give directions

rescue kids

wake up early

take pictures

ride a camel

Actress

sleep late

put on makeup

sign autographs

*See list on page 9.

Rap in the Real World

A. Conversation. With a partner, answer these questions.

- What are you doing now?
- What are your classmates doing now?
- What do you usually do on weekends?

B. Discussion. In small groups, answer these questions.

- What is happening in the news these days?
- What is happening in your country these days?
- Describe some American customs and some customs from your culture.

Example: People in the United States usually shake hands. People in my culture bow. They don't usually hug.

By the Way . . .

There are some verbs that are often used with this structure: *go (+ verb)+ing*.
Use this structure with the simple present but not the present continuous.

Examples: I go fishing every weekend.
I am fishing right now.

Some of these verbs are:

dance	fish	swim	hike	shop	sightsee
ski	water ski	skate	ice-skate	surf	sail
rock-climb	skin-dive	scuba dive	sky dive	snorkel	bowl
hang glide	jog	hunt	job-hunt	house-hunt	sunbathe

Non-Action Verbs

The verbs in the column on the left are usually NON-ACTION Verbs; that is, they are *not usually used in any of the continuous tenses*. However, many of these verbs have two meanings; one NON-ACTION and the other ACTION.

VERBS	NON-ACTION	ACTION
Condition:		
be	He is tall.	He's being very good. (be = BEHAVE/ACT)
consist	It consists of eggs and milk.	
cost	This costs too much.	
equal	Two and four equal six.	
fit	The suit fits well.	The tailor is fitting him for a new suit. (fit = MEASURE FOR; CAUSE TO FIT OR CONFORM)
match	Her purse matches her shoes. (match = LOOK ATTRACTIVE WITH)	
matter	It doesn't matter.	
owe	I owe him $10.00.	
resemble	She resembles her sister.	
weigh	He weighs 150 lbs.	He's weighing himself now. (weigh = PUT ON A SCALE)

Verbs	Non-Action	Action
Possession:		
belong	That belongs to them.	
contain	This contains our dishes.	

have	I have a typewriter.
	    (have = POSSESS)
		I'm having some problems.
		    (have = EXPERIENCE)
		 He's having breakfast.
		    (have = EAT/DRINK)

own	They own some property.	
possess	He possesses two houses.	
Perception:		

appear	He appears to be ready.
	    (appear = SEEM)
		She's appearing in a new play.
		    (appear = PERFORM or COME
		    INTO SIGHT)

feel	I feel it's a good idea.
	    (feel = THINK/BELIEVE)
	 He feels relieved.
	    (feel = HAVE AN EMOTION)
		I'm feeling better now.
		    (feel = EXPERIENCE AN EMOTION OR
		    PHYSICAL FEELING)
		 She's feeling around for the
		 light switch.
		    (feel = TOUCH)

hear	He doesn't hear you.
	    (hear = PERCEIVE WITH THE EARS)
		You'll be hearing from my lawyer.
		    (hear = GET A LETTER OR CALL)
		 Judge Burr is hearing this case.
		    (hear = JUDGE; LISTEN TO TESTIMONY)

look	You look tired.
	    (look = SEEM)
		He's looking at you.
		    (look = USE ONE'S EYES)

see	I see him over there.
	    (see = PERCEIVE WITH THE EYES)
		The mayor is seeing her now.
		    (see = MEET WITH)

seem	It seems like a good idea.	

smell	This smells good!
	    (smell = HAVE A SMELL)
	 I smell something odd.
	    (smell = PERCEIVE A SMELL
	    INVOLUNTARILY)
		She's smelling every perfume in the
		 store.
		    (smell = SNIFF)

sound	That sounds good.
	    (sound = SEEM)
		They're sounding the alarm.
		    (sound = CAUSE A SOUND)

taste	This tastes great!
	    (taste = HAVE A TASTE)
	 I taste something strange.
	    (taste = PERCEIVE A TASTE
	    INVOLUNTARILY)
		He's tasting your cake now.
		    (taste = TRY, SAMPLE FOOD)

VERBS	NON-ACTION	ACTION
Emotional/ Mental Activity		
appreciate	I appreciate your suggestion.	
approve	He doesn't approve.	
believe	I believe her.	
desire	She desired to see them once again. (formal)	
dislike	I dislike being in crowds.	
doubt	He doubts that it's true.	
guess	I guess we should start. (guess = SUPPOSE)	He doesn't know for sure. He's just guessing. (guess = MAKE AN ESTIMATE)
hate	I hate this music.	
imagine	I imagine that you're tired. (imagine = GUESS, THINK)	You're just imagining things. (imagine = USE THE IMAGINATION)
know	She knows the president.	
like	We like to ski.	
love	They love their country.	I'm loving this! (love = ENJOY; used as slang)
mean	It means "no." (mean = SIGNIFY)	I've been meaning to do that. (mean = INTEND)
mind	I don't mind. (mind = OBJECT TO)	Who's minding the store? (mind = TAKE CARE OF)
need*	We need a car.	
prefer	He prefers this one.	
recognize	I don't recognize anyone.	
remember	They don't remember anything.	
think	I think it's too big. (think = BELIEVE, HAVE AN OPINION)	Wait a second. I'm thinking. (think = CONSIDER, REFLECT)
understand	I understand what you're saying.	
want*	I don't want any right now.	

***Note:** Although these verbs are not usually used with continuous tenses, they are frequently used with the **past perfect continuous** and **present perfect continuous**.

I've *been needing* a new coat for a long time.

He *had been wanting* that car for a long time when he finally bought it.

Figure It Out

Practice: Action and Non-action Verbs. Decide the meaning of each verb in parentheses; use pages 9–11 to help you with this. Write the meaning in the box. Then fill in the tense—**present continuous** for action verbs and **simple present** for non-action verbs. (Everything is happening *now*.)

1. He _____is having_____ (have = | experience |) a good time.

2. That actor _____ (appear = | |) in a movie that we saw last night.

3. I _____ (guess = | |) this isn't the right answer.

4. They _____ (have = | |) some tea.

5. That _____ (sound = | |) like a bad idea.

6. What _____ you _____ (think = | |)? Do you like it?

7. This furniture polish _____ (smell = | |) like lemon.

8. The doctor _____ (see = | |) a patient right now, but she can call you back in a few minutes.

9. _____ you _____ (mind = | |) if I open a window?

10. She _____ (weigh = | |) the tomatoes.

Fill It In

Tenses in Context. Fill in the blanks in the following story with the **simple present** or **present continuous** tense. A check mark (✓) indicates that more than one tense may be possible in some of the blanks.

The Fishing Trip

Gordon and his three sons, Mark, Joe, and Leo, (1)_____ (own) a charter fishing boat. Every day when they (2)_____ (sail), they (3)_____ (take) a boat full of would-be fishermen out to sea. Leo, the youngest, (4)_____ (sell) tickets every afternoon for the next day's trip. The passengers (5)_____ (arrive) now with high hopes. Some (6)_____ (carry) their own equipment, and others (7)_____ (rent) it from Gordon.

Usually when everyone (8)_____ (be) aboard, Gordon (9)_____ (stand) at the wheel and (10)_____ (signal) Mark to untie the boat. But today Mark (11)_____ (daydream), so Joe (12)_____ (loosen) the rope and (13)_____ (throw) it on the boat. Gordon always (14)_____ (start) the motor while Joe (15)_____✓ (prepare) the bait. On the way out, Leo sometimes (16)_____ (give) the fishermen ideas on how to fish. When Gordon (17)_____ (find) a good spot, Leo (18)_____ (drop) anchor and the fishermen (19)_____ (throw) out their lines.

Today, they (20)_____ (fish) in one of Gordon's favorite spots. Gordon (21)_____ (tell) his favorite fish stories. Some of the passengers (22)_____ (eat) their lunch, while others, who (23)_____✓ (not feel) well, (24)_____ (try) not to look at the food or smell the bait. One of the fishermen (25)_____ (reel) in a fish. His friend (26)_____ (take) his picture.

Leo and Joe (27)_____ (help) some of the passengers bait their hooks. Mark (28)_____ (also try) to help. Poor Mark! He (29)_____ (always try) to be useful, but usually (30)_____ (end up) causing some damage. He (31)_____ (forever trip) over ropes, (32)_____ (fall) over the anchor, or (33)_____ (get) tangled in the fishermen's lines. At this moment, while his brothers (34)_____✓ (help) the passengers, Mark (35)_____ (lean) out of the boat to catch one of the fishermen's stubborn fish with his net. The fish (36)_____ (jump) in all directions. Oh, oh, it (37)_____ (seem) that the fish (38)_____ (win). Mark (39)_____ (fall) overboard. He never (40)_____ (know) when to give up.

Read the story on the left. When you finish, go back to the beginning, cover up the story on the left, and choose the correct tense for each capitalized simple form of the verb to the right of the picture.

It's Elmer Kadiddle's 100th birthday today.

It BE Elmer Kadiddle's 100th birthday today.

Elmer *has* never *been* sick a day in his life. He *has* never *taken* any medicine or *been* to any doctors.

Elmer NEVER BE sick a day in his life. He NEVER TAKE any medicine or BE to any doctors.

Elmer *lives* on a farm in Nebraska.

Elmer LIVE on a farm in Nebraska.

He's *lived* on the same farm since he was born.

He LIVE on the same farm since he was born.

Elmer *has gotten up* at sunrise every day of his life. He*'s fed* the chickens and *gathered* the eggs since he was old enough to walk.

Elmer GET UP at sunrise every day of his life. He FEED the chickens and GATHER the eggs since he was old enough to walk.

He*'s milked* the cows without missing a day—even his wedding day.

He MILK the cows without missing a day—even his wedding day.

Elmer *has been* married to the same woman for the last 80 years.

Elmer BE married to the same woman for the last 80 years.

His wife, Iona, *grows* all their vegetables in her garden.

His wife, Iona, GROW all their vegetables in her garden.

She *cans* fruits and vegetables, and every day she *bakes* her own bread.

She CAN fruits and vegetables, and every day she BAKE her own bread.

Iona and Elmer *have been* happily married since their wedding day. Their only arguments *have been* about their son, Elmer, Jr.

Iona and Elmer BE happily married since their wedding day. Their only arguments BE about their son, Elmer, Jr.

Junior *is* nothing like his father. He *hates* farm life.

Elmer *complains* that Junior *has* never *done* a day's work in his life.

Junior usually *gets up* at noon, and his mother always *has* a big breakfast waiting for him.

After breakfast, he often *goes* fishing.

But he *doesn't* catch very many fish.

Junior *spends* Saturday nights playing the guitar for his friends.

Junior BE nothing like his father. He HATE farm life.

Elmer COMPLAIN that Junior NEVER DO a day's work in his life.

Junior usually GET UP at noon, and his mother always HAVE a big breakfast waiting for him.

After breakfast, he often GO fishing.

But he NOT CATCH very many fish.

Junior SPEND Saturday nights playing the guitar for his friends.

He *has dreamed* about going to the big city since he was a young boy.

But, as Elmer *says*, there *is* no need to worry; Junior *is* so lazy that he would never pack a suitcase.

Elmer and Iona *have argued* about this *again* and again for years.

Elmer *says* it*'s* time for the boy to settle down and get to work.

Iona *says* to give him time; he*'s* just a boy. After all, he*'s* barely 59 years old.

THE END

He DREAM about going to the big city since he was a young boy.

But, as Elmer SAY, there BE no need to worry; Junior BE so lazy that he would never pack a suitcase.

Elmer and Iona ARGUE about this again and again for years.

Elmer SAY it BE time for the boy to settle down and get to work.

Iona SAY to give him time; he BE just a boy. After all, he BE barely 59 years old.

PRESENT PERFECT	SIMPLE PRESENT
1. One use of the **present perfect** is to express an activity happening *now*. Something in the sentence or context tells us when the action began. The action may be continuous or periodic.	With the **simple present**, there is no indication of when the action began or how long it has gone on.

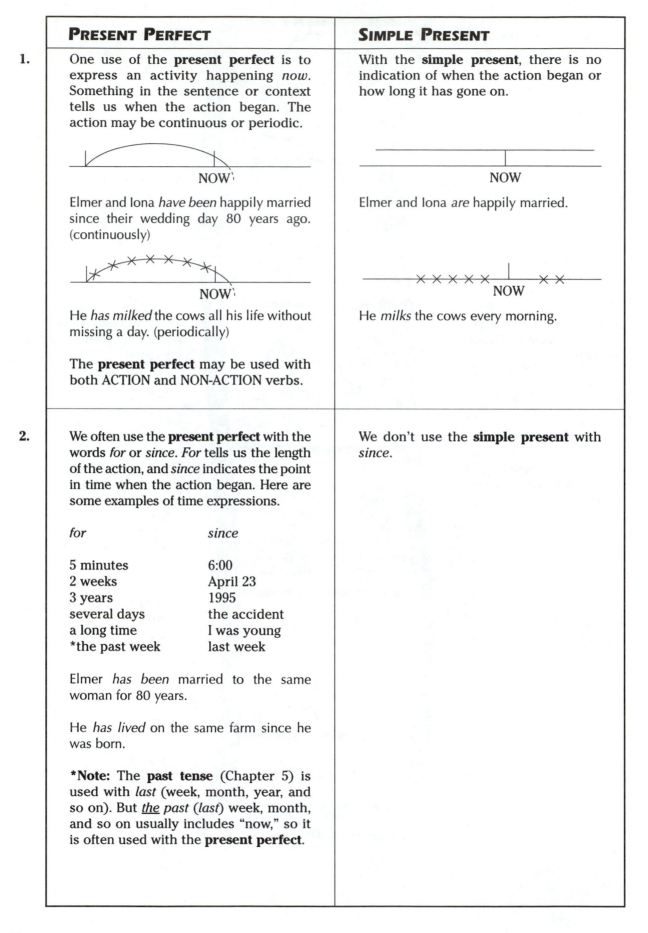

PRESENT PERFECT	SIMPLE PRESENT
Elmer and Iona *have been* happily married since their wedding day 80 years ago. (continuously)	Elmer and Iona *are* happily married.

PRESENT PERFECT	SIMPLE PRESENT
He *has milked* the cows all his life without missing a day. (periodically) The **present perfect** may be used with both ACTION and NON-ACTION verbs.	He *milks* the cows every morning.

PRESENT PERFECT	SIMPLE PRESENT
2. We often use the **present perfect** with the words *for* or *since*. *For* tells us the length of the action, and *since* indicates the point in time when the action began. Here are some examples of time expressions.	We don't use the **simple present** with *since*.

for	since
5 minutes	6:00
2 weeks	April 23
3 years	1995
several days	the accident
a long time	I was young
*the past week	last week

Elmer *has been* married to the same woman for 80 years.

He *has lived* on the same farm since he was born.

*Note: The **past tense** (Chapter 5) is used with *last* (week, month, year, and so on). But <u>the</u> past (*last*) week, month, and so on usually includes "now," so it is often used with the **present perfect**.

PRESENT PERFECT	
Iona *was* sick *last week.*	
Iona *has been* sick for *the last week.*	
We also use the **present perfect** with expressions such as:	
all day (week, year, and so on) so far up until now all (his/her/my/and so on) life	
Junior *has hated* the farm all his life.	

3. When we have a compound verb, the verb *have* is omitted from the second action.

He*'s fed* the chickens and *gathered* eggs since he was old enough to walk.

For other uses of the **present perfect**, see Chapter 5.

Rap It Up

Oral Practice. Work with a partner. For each picture on this page, make up two logical sentences. In the first, tell what people do every day. In the second, tell *for how long* or *since when* they have done these things. Use the time expressions in the column at the right in the second sentence. Make as many sentences as you can.

Example: Elmer is a farmer.
He's been a farmer for a long time.

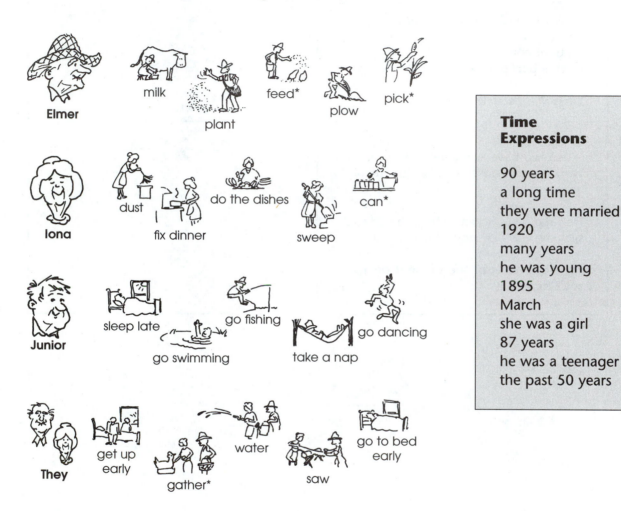

Time Expressions

90 years
a long time
they were married
1920
many years
he was young
1895
March
she was a girl
87 years
he was a teenager
the past 50 years

*These verbs are transitive. (They must have an object.)

Rap in the Real World

A. Conversation. With a partner, talk about your life. Use as many of the verbs from the exercise above as possible and add verbs of your own. Use the **simple present** and the **present perfect** tenses.

Examples: I get up early every day. I've gotten up at 7:00 every day for the past five years. I've never milked a cow, but sometimes I pick flowers in our garden.

B. Discussion. Choose a friend or family member who has a very different life from yours. In small groups, tell your classmates about your life and this person's life.

Picture Puzzle

Tenses in Context. On another piece of paper, write out the following story. Change all of the pictures and symbols to words. The character's name [🕴] is Norbert (Elmer's brother), but you should use pronouns (*he, him*) whenever possible. For each of the circled verbs, choose the **simple present** or the **present perfect**. In a few cases, more than one tense may be possible. If you can't guess the meaning of a symbol, check page 164 in the Appendix.

Norbert's Life

ELMER'S BROTHER, [🕴], (BE) 97 & (LIVE) ALONE [X] THE [city]. [🕴] (LIVE) THERE SINCE [🕴] LEFT THE [farmhouse] 75 YEARS AGO. [🕴] (HAVE) AN APARTMENT [△] THE TOP FLOOR OF A [building] FOR THE PAST 20 YEARS.

[🕴] (BE) A VERY CHARMING PERSON, SO [🕴] (HAVE) A LOT OF FRIENDS & (LEAD) A BUSY LIFE. [🕴] ALMOST NEVER (GET) [↑] OF [bed] BEFORE [clock] EACH [sun] BECAUSE [🕴] USUALLY (STAY) ↑ LATE AT [moon]. [🕴] (LIKE) → PLAY [cards] W/ HIS FRIENDS [X] THE AFTER [clock]. SOMETIMES [🕴] (GO) → THE [horse] RACES, & [🕴] ALWAYS (WIN) A LOT OF [$]. [X] THE [P.M.] [🕴] USUALLY (TAKE) HIS [girlfriend] → AN [$↑] RESTAURANT. [🕴] (KNOW) [woman] FOR [□] 30 YEARS, BUT [🕴] (FEEL) THAT [🕴] (BE) READY → GET MARRIED.

[🕴] (KNOW) THAT MANY [people] (SPEND) EVERY AFTER [clock] [X] THE [park], WHERE THEY (SIT) A [bench] & (FEED) THE [bird]s. BUT [🕴] (NEVER GO) [X]→ THE [park] SINCE [🕴] CAME → THE [city] BECAUSE [🕴] (THINK) THAT ONLY ELDERLY [people] (GO) → [park]s.

EVERY SUMMER, [🕴] (TAKE) A [train] ↓ → HIS BROTHER'S [farm] & (SPEND) SOME TIME THERE. [🕴] (BE) THERE RIGHT NOW. [🕴] (ONLY BE) THERE FOR 5 [sun]s, BUT [🕴] (BE) READY → GO BACK → THE [city].

[🕴] & HIS BROTHER ELMER (BE) VERY DIFFERENT FROM EACH OTHER, & THEY (ARGUE) ABOUT EVERYTHING EVER SINCE [🕴] ARRIVED [△] TUESDAY. THE PROBLEM (BE) THAT [🕴] (NEVER LIKE) THE LIFE OF A FARMER. [🕴] (COMPLAIN) FOR 4 DAYS ABOUT GETTING ↑ AT [sunrise] ↑ & HELPING ELMER W/ THE [cow]s. [🕴] (FEED) THE [chicken]s & (GATHER) 08 ALL WEEK, BUT [🕴] (ENJOY) IT. THE TRUTH (BE) THAT [🕴] (HATE) ANIMALS. [🕴] (THINK) THAT [horse]s (BELONG) [X] THE RACES & [bird]s (BELONG) [X] THE [park], & [🕴] (BE) SURE THAT [people] (BELONG) [X] A [city]!

ELMER'S WIFE, IONA, (BE) WORRIED ABOUT 🏃's HEALTH FOR MANY YEARS. SHE

(FEED) 🏃 HOMEMADE SOUP & FRESH 🥖 ALL WEEK, & SHE (MAKE) 🏃 GO → 🛏 AT

9:00 EVERY 🌙. 🏃's WORST PROBLEM (BE) THAT SHE (TRY) SINCE TUESDAY → PERSUADE

🏃 → SETTLE ↓ & GET MARRIED → HIS 👰. 🏃 (HEAR) THIS FROM HER FOR MANY

YEARS. EVERY TIME, 🏃 (SIGH) & (TELL) HER THE SAME THING: THAT 🏃 (BE) A

BACHELOR ALL HIS LIFE, & 🏃 (WANT) → CHANGE NOW.

PRESENT PERFECT CONTINUOUS
PRESENT CONTINUOUS

Read the story on the left. When you finish, go back to the beginning, cover up the story on the left, and choose the correct tense for each capitalized simple form of the verb to the right of the picture.

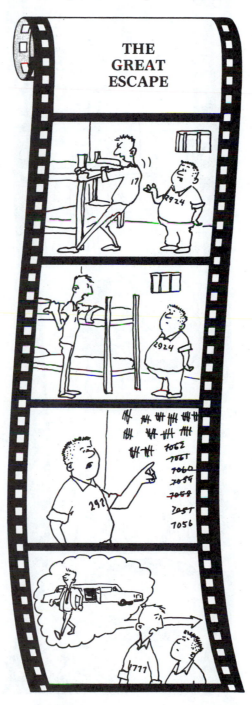

—Hey, Joey, what *are* you *doing*?

—I*'m getting* ready to say good-bye to this place.

—Ha, that's a good one! You know you have another 15 years to spend in here.

—Yeah, but I*'ve been thinking* that on the outside, those could be the best 15 years of my life. So I*'m getting* out of here now.

—Hey, Joey, what you DO?

—I GET ready to say good-bye to this place.

—Ha, that's a good one! You know you have another 15 years to spend in here.

—Yeah, but I THINK that on the outside, those could be the best 15 years of my life. So I GET out of here now.

For the last three months, Shorty, I *'ve been digging* a tunnel.

—No kidding! Where *have* you *been digging* this tunnel?

—It starts under the bunk in my cell and goes out beyond the main gate.

For the last few days I *'ve been trying* to finish the last part of the tunnel, but I *'m having* a lot of trouble.

—What's the trouble, Joey?

—It*'s been going* too slowly since Lefty stopped helping. I need a strong partner to help me.

For the last three months, Shorty, I DIG a tunnel.

—No kidding! Where you DIG this tunnel?

—It starts under the bunk in my cell and goes out beyond the main gate.

For the last few days I TRY to finish the last part of the tunnel, but I HAVE a lot of trouble.

—What's the trouble, Joey?

—It GO too slowly since Lefty stopped helping. I need a strong partner to help me.

—No problem, Joey. I'm strong. By the way, what *have* you *been doing* with the dirt, anyway?

—Well, Shorty, you know you*'ve been complaining* the last few months about the food tasting strange. Well, there's a reason for that.

—Oh, no, Joey, not that!
—Too late to worry about it now, pal! Come on. Let's get in the tunnel.

—Even on the eggs, Joey? Is that why the eggs *have been tasting* funny?

—Hurry up! The guards *are coming*.

—We*'ve been crawling* for an awfully long time, Joey. Are you sure we*'re going* in the right direction?

—No problem, Joey. I'm strong. By the way, what you DO with the dirt, anyway?

—Well, Shorty, you know you COMPLAIN the last few months about the food tasting strange. Well, there's a reason for that.

—Oh, no, Joey, not that!
—Too late to worry about it now, pal! Come on. Let's get in the tunnel.

—Even on the eggs, Joey? Is that why the eggs TASTE funny?

—Hurry up! The guards COME.

—We CRAWL for an awfully long time, Joey. Are you sure we GO in the right direction?

—I'm positive. *I've been using* this map that Lefty gave me before he left.

—I'm positive. I USE this map that Lefty gave me before he left.

This is it. This is what*'s been giving* me trouble for the past week.

This is it. This is what GIVE me trouble for the past week.

—No problem, Joey, give me a hand.

—No problem, Joey, give me a hand.

—Come on, Shorty. We*'re getting* closer.

—Come on, Shorty. We GET closer.

—Well, hello, boys. *I've been waiting* for you to show up.

—Well, hello, boys. I WAIT for you to show up.

THE END

PRESENT PERFECT CONTINUOUS	PRESENT CONTINUOUS

1. The **present perfect continuous**, like the **present perfect**, expresses an action that began in the past and is continuing *now*. The action may be continuous or periodic.

```
       _____
      |                   \
   2:00                  NOW
```

She's been waiting since 2:00. (continuously)

```
      _×_×_×_×_×_×_×_×_×_
     |×                  |
                        NOW
```

For the last three months, I*'ve been digging* a tunnel. (periodically; a little bit each day)

Sometimes the indication of when the action began is not in the sentence. It's only in the mind of the speaker.

I*'ve been waiting* for you to show up.

Exception: We often use the **present perfect continuous** for a finished action if:

a. the action ended very close to "now"

   and

b. we want to emphasize long duration or hardship.

Oh, there you are! I*'ve been looking* for you everywhere!

The **present continuous** also expresses an action happening *now*, but there is no indication of when it began.

```
   _____|___
                          NOW
```

She's waiting over there.

PRESENT PERFECT CONTINUOUS	**PRESENT CONTINUOUS**
2. The **present perfect continuous** is not used with NON-ACTION verbs (see pages 9–11) or with frequency adverbs such as *never, often,* and *always.* The **present perfect** is used instead. (See the practice exercises at the end of this chapter.)	The **present continuous** is not usually used with NON-ACTION verbs or with adverbs of frequency. The **simple present** is used instead. (See Chapter 1 for examples.) The **present continuous** is occasionally used (with an adverb of frequency) for an action in progress when another action happens. The verb in the **present continuous** may stop when the second action occurs, or it may continue beyond the second action. NOW Joey *is* usually *lying* in his bunk when the lights go out every night.
3. We often use the **present perfect continuous** with such words and expressions as: since for all day (week, month, and so on) in the past week (few months, year, few years, and so on) recently, lately I*'ve been digging* a tunnel for the last three months. (See Chapter 2 for more on *since* and *for.*)	The **present continuous** is not usually used with these words and expressions. (For other uses of the **present continuous**, see Chapter 15.)
4. When we have a compound verb, the verbs HAVE and BEEN are omitted from the second action. He*'s been thinking* about his future and *making* plans.	

Rap It Up

Oral Practice. Work with a partner. Look at the pictures below and take turns asking and answering questions about what the people are doing.

Examples:
  A: What is the man in cell #6 doing?
  B: He's sawing the bars on the window.
  A: How long has he been sawing?
  B: He's been sawing since this morning.

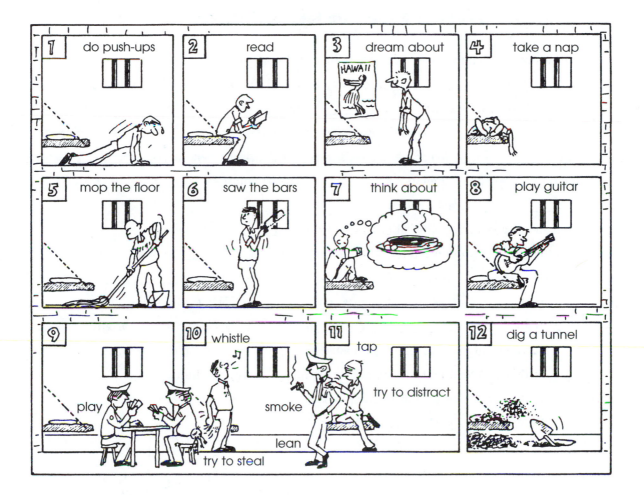

1. do push-ups
2. read
3. dream about   HAWAII
4. take a nap
5. mop the floor
6. saw the bars
7. think about
8. play guitar
9. play
10. whistle   try to steal   lean
11. smoke   tap   try to distract
12. dig a tunnel

Rap in the Real World

Role Play. Work with a partner. Take the roles of the people in one of the pairs below. You have not seen each other for a long time. Make up a conversation. Use the **present continuous** and **present perfect continuous** tenses.

        two neighbors   doctor and patient
        two friends   ex-husband and wife

Example:
  A: Hi, Susan, how are you? What have you been doing?
  B: Hello, Jerry, I'm fine. I've been . . . And you?
  A: I've been . . .

Fill It In

Tenses in Context. Fill in the blanks in the following story with the **present perfect continuous** or the **present continuous** tense. Remember a check mark (✓) indicates that more than one tense may be possible in some of the blanks.

Joey and Shorty are still in prison. One of the prison guards is now making his monthly report on the prisoners to the warden.

Progress Report on Joey and Shorty

—Guard, how are the two prisoners, Joey and Shorty, doing?

—Well, Warden, Shorty (1)_____ (do) very well lately. He is practically a model prisoner. He (2)_____ ✓ (work) very hard. He (3)_____ (always volunteer) for the jobs that no one wants to do. He (4)_____ (constantly sweep) the floors and (5)_____ (clean) the cells. For months he (6)_____ (do) some of Joey's jobs. For the past week, he (7)_____ (work) in the prison kitchen in place of Joey; he (8)_____ (peel) potatoes, (9)_____ (chop) onions, and (10)_____ (wash) the dishes.

—That's excellent, guard, but what about Joey? How (11)_____ ✓ (Joey do)?

—Joey is not exactly a model prisoner. At the moment he (12)_____ (work) on three different plans that we know of to escape from prison. For months now he (13)_____ (try) to build a ladder with anything he can. His friends (14)_____ ✓ (bring) him pieces of sticks, blankets, and even socks. Joey (15)_____ ✓ (use) these to make a ladder. The poor guy (16)_____ ✓ (stay up) nights to make his unusual ladder. What he doesn't know is that we (17)_____ ✓ (only wait) for him to finish before we take it away from him.

Something else that he . . . why, look, warden, what is that commotion over there? That guard (18)_____ (look) inside a garbage can. I think he (19)_____ (talk) to someone. Look, he (20)_____ (pull) Joey out of the garbage can. I'm sure Joey (21)_____ ✓ (try) to escape again. He (22)_____ (try) to get thrown out with the garbage since February. He (23)_____ (always look) for a way to get out. For years now he (24)_____ (bribe) the guards, (25)_____ (steal) keys, and (26)_____ (saw) the bars to try to escape.

—Thank you, guard. I'm going to write all this in a letter to the judge. Maybe Joey's going to stay with us longer than he thinks.

By the Way . . .

Do *not* use the **present perfect continuous** if there is:

- a non-action verb (pages 9–11)
- a number of times (twice, five times, many times, etc.)
- a frequency adverb (never, often, always, etc.)
- a *specific* amount of money or weight ($135.00, 55 pounds, etc.)

Instead, use the **present perfect** in these cases.

Examples: INCORRECT: He's often *been dreaming* of getting out. (frequency adverb)

              CORRECT: He's often *dreamed* of getting out.

                       He's *been dreaming* for a long time of getting out.

              INCORRECT: She's *been making* $2,000 in the stock market. (specific amount)

              CORRECT: She's *made* $2,000 in the stock market.

                       She's *been making* a lot of money in the stock market.

Figure It Out

Read the following **incorrect** sentences. Why is the tense in each sentence incorrect? Write the reason on the line. Then correct the tense on a separate piece of paper. (There are two possible ways to correct some sentences.)

1. Joey *has been trying* to escape twice. _number of times (twice)_

     Joey has tried to escape twice.

     Joey has been trying to escape all year.

2. Shorty *has been owing* Joey money for five months. _____

3. He's *been losing* fifteen pounds. _____

4. Joey's cousin *has* never *been visiting* him. _____

5. He *has been spending* $15 on phone calls this month. _____

6. Joey and Shorty *have been knowing* each other for three years. _____

7. The warden *has* often *been catching* prisoners escaping. _____

8. He's *been seeming* tired. _____

9. They've *been digging* a tunnel three times. _____

10. Joey *has been saving* $25 this month. _____

4 PRESENT TENSE REVIEW

Fill in the blanks with the following tenses. In some cases (✓), more than one tense is possible.

Simple Present

Present Continuous

Present Perfect

Present Perfect Continuous

Friday Afternoon at MacGruder's Department Store

It's a normal Friday afternoon at MacGruder's Department Store. At this moment in the shoe department, a young man and his wife (1)_____ (try) to buy new shoes for their three small children. The kids (2)_____ (wiggle) and (3)_____ (scream) and (4)_____ (chase) each other around. The salesman, George, (5)_____ ✓ (go) crazy. He (6)_____ ✓ (wait on) the family for the past hour, with no success. Either the shoes (7)_____ (not fit), or the children's father (8)_____ (think) they're too expensive.

Over at the jewelry counter, Julie (9)_____ ✓ (have) a hard time, too. She (10)_____ ✓ (run) back and forth all afternoon. One lady (11)_____ ✓ (try on) earrings for twenty-five minutes and (12)_____ ✓ (not put) them back on the rack, so now there is a mountain of earrings on the counter.

Beth Ellen, the store detective, (13)_____ ✓ (walk) slowly around the store since she arrived at 10:00. Her feet (14)_____ ✓ (kill) her. Every day, she (15)_____ (walk) around and (16)_____ (try) to look like a normal shopper while she (17)_____ ✓ (do) her job catching shoplifters. Unfortunately, Beth Ellen (18)_____ (not catch) a single shoplifter in the past year because she can't see well, and she (19)_____ (refuse) to wear glasses.

Up in his office right now, Mr. MacGruder (20)_____ (stand) by a small window which (21)_____ (look) out over the first floor of his store. He (22)_____ (see) a customer at the jewelry counter secretly putting expensive earrings into her purse. Beth Ellen (23)_____ (walk) right past her at this very moment, but of course she (24)_____ (not see) the woman steal the earrings because she (25)_____ (not wear) her glasses. Mr. MacGruder's face (26)_____ (begin) to turn purple, and now he (27)_____ (tear) out his hair. He (28)_____ ✓ (regret) hiring Beth Ellen as the store detective ever since his sister persuaded him to, but he can't do anything about it because the girl (29)_____ (be) his niece.

Finish the Story

Use the phrases and pictures on this page to help you rewrite the story of MacGruder's Department Store. **Do not look back at the original story**. Your story will have four paragraphs—one for each of the pictures below. Your story won't be exactly the same as the original, but you should correctly use the four tenses from this chapter: **present continuous, simple present, present perfect,** and **present perfect continuous**. The verbs on this page are in either picture form or the simple form.

Cue Sheet

1. try to buy
   wiggle/scream/chase
   wait on (for an hour)
   not fit
   go crazy

2. have a hard time
   run back and forth
   try on (for 25 minutes)
   not put back

3. walk slowly
   (since she arrived)
   feet—kill
   try to look like
   not catch a single shoplifter
   refuse to wear

4. stand
   look
   see a customer
   Beth Ellen walk/not see/not wear
   turn purple
   tear out his hair
   regret—since
   the girl be

Friday Afternoon at MacGruder's Department Store

In the shoe department of MacGruder's Department Store, a man and woman are trying to buy shoes for their kids. . .

Story Lines

Use these Story Lines to help you answer the questions on the next page. The verbs on this page are all in the simple form, but you'll choose the correct tenses.

Friday Night

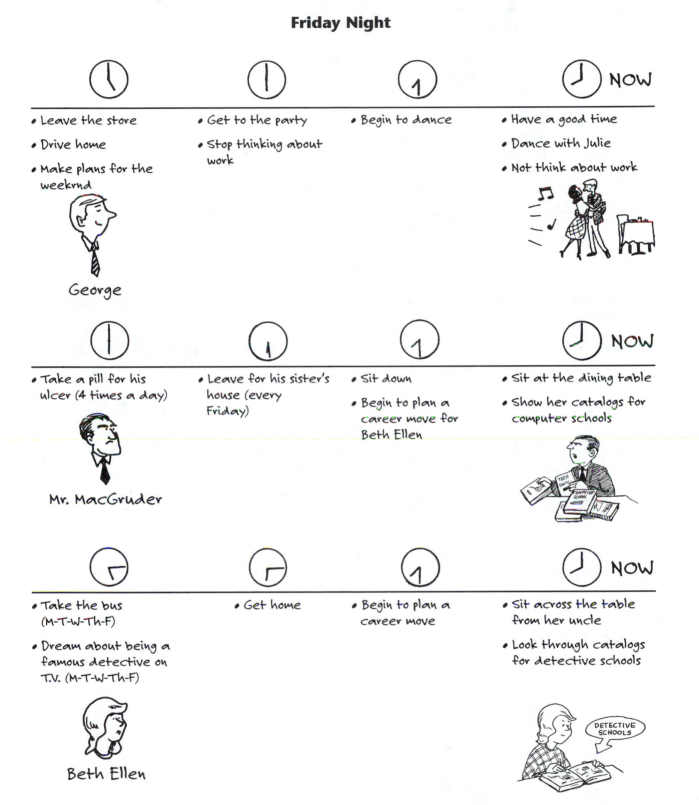

George

- Leave the store
- Drive home
- Make plans for the weekrnd

- Get to the party
- Stop thinking about work

- Begin to dance

NOW
- Have a good time
- Dance with Julie
- Not think about work

Mr. MacGruder

- Take a pill for his ulcer (4 times a day)

- Leave for his sister's house (every Friday)

- Sit down
- Begin to plan a career move for Beth Ellen

NOW
- Sit at the dining table
- Show her catalogs for computer schools

Beth Ellen

- Take the bus (M-T-W-Th-F)
- Dream about being a famous detective on T.V. (M-T-W-Th-F)

- Get home

- Begin to plan a career move

NOW
- Sit across the table from her uncle
- Look through catalogs for detective schools

DETECTIVE SCHOOLS

Look at the Story Lines on the previous page and answer these questions. Be sure to use the same tenses as in the questions.

1. What's George doing right now?
2. How long has he been at the party?
3. How long has he been off work?
4. Why is he having a good time?
5. Has he thought about work this evening? (*since/for*)
6. What time does he usually leave work?
7. When does he make plans for the weekend? (*while*)
8. Where is Mr. MacGruder sitting?
9. What's he doing?
10. Why is he planning a career move for Beth Ellen?
11. How often does he have dinner at his sister's?
12. How often does he take pills for his ulcer?
13. Why do you think he has an ulcer?
14. How does Beth Ellen usually get home?
15. What does she do at that time?
16. What's she doing? What else?

It's Your Turn. Use the **present continuous, simple present, present perfect,** and **present perfect continuous** in the following exercises.

A. Choose 2 or 3 people (or groups of people) from the list below. Write one paragraph about each. Use your imagination! What are these people doing? What do they usually do? How long have they been doing these things?

a famous movie star	a famous athlete
someone in your family	the president (prime minister,
the people in your country	king, queen) of your country
your teacher	an astronaut

B. Pretend you are a television news reporter. You're giving a live report from the scene of an event happening right now. Describe the event to a partner. Choose one of the following situations/events:

a fashion show	a battle	a stunt on a movie set
a movie premiere	a flood	a sports event

PAST

Read the story on the left. When you finish, go back to the beginning, cover up the story on the left, and choose the correct tense for each capitalized simple form of the verb to the right of the picture.

THE
SNOB

—This is certainly a nice party, isn't it?

—This is certainly a nice party, isn't it?

—Oh, it's all right, but last week I *attended* an elegant party on the royal yacht.

—Oh, it's all right, but last week I ATTEND an elegant party on the royal yacht.

Actually, I*'ve been* to so many of these parties lately that they*'ve become* quite a bore.

Actually, I BE to so many of these parties lately that they BECOME quite a bore.

—Maybe you need a good vacation. *Have* you ever *gone* up to Lake Gorgeous? It's quite nice this year. We*'ve been* there twice.

—Maybe you need a good vacation. You ever GO up to Lake Gorgeous? It's quite nice this year. We BE there twice.

—Oh, yes, I know. Our family *has owned* that lake for generations.

—On our last vacation we *spent* most of our time fishing.

—I*'ve* never *liked* fishing, but I*'ve* just *returned* from a shark-hunting trip. I found it exciting—well, almost exciting.

—Speaking of excitement, I*'ve* recently *learned* how to fly a plane.

—Oh, I*'ve* often *flown* our jumbo jet myself. Why, just last week I *flew* it across the Atlantic.

—I*'ve* always *found* swimming a nice way to relax.

—Oh, yes, I know. Our family OWN that lake for generations.

—On our last vacation we SPEND most of our time fishing.

—I never LIKE fishing, but I just RETURN from a shark-hunting trip. I FIND it exciting—well, almost exciting.

—Speaking of excitement, I recently LEARN how to fly a plane.

—Oh, I often FLY our jumbo jet myself. Why, just last week I FLY it across the Atlantic.

—I always FIND swimming a nice way to relax.

—I've gotten tired of
swimming. Last year
we went diving for pearls.
That was a bit more
interesting.

—That reminds me. My
husband bought me a
beautiful string of pearls
for my birthday.

—My husband has already
bought me so much jewelry
that last April he decided to
trade it all in on a diamond
mine.

—Oh, it was in April that we
bought our new house. It's a
roomy four-bedroom place
with a swimming pool.

—We've bought two homes
this year. The first was too
small; it had only 25 rooms.

The second one is
more comfortable. We've
just built a large indoor
swimming pool in addition
to the one outside.

—I GET tired of swimming.
Last year we GO diving for
pearls. That BE a bit more
interesting.

—That reminds me. My
husband BUY me a beautiful
string of pearls for my
birthday.

—My husband already BUY
me so much jewelry that
last April he DECIDE to
trade it all in on a diamond
mine.

—Oh, it BE in April that we
BUY our new house. It's a
roomy four-bedroom place
with a swimming pool.

—We BUY two homes this
year. The first BE too small;
it HAVE only 25 rooms.

The second one is more
comfortable. We just BUILD
a large indoor swimming
pool in addition to the one
outside.

—How many rooms *did* you *say* it had?

—I have no idea. I *haven't seen* all of the rooms yet.

I*'ve had* a lot of house guests in the last few months.

—I*'ve* always *enjoyed* the company of good friends.

—Oh, yes, in the past few years I*'ve acquired* a large circle of friends all around the world. My goodness! Where *has* everyone *gone*?

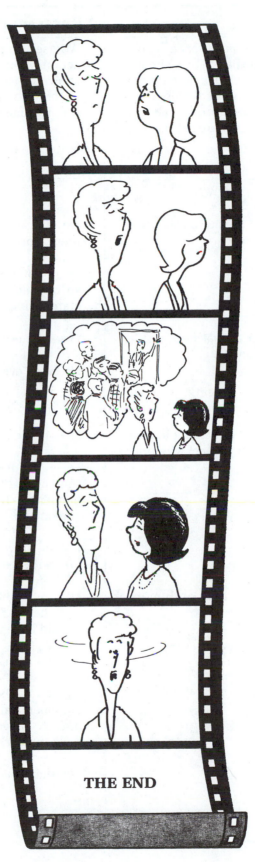

THE END

—How many rooms you SAY it had?

—I have no idea. I NOT SEE all of the rooms yet.

I HAVE a lot of house guests in the last few months.

—I always ENJOY the company of good friends.

—Oh, yes, in the past few years I ACQUIRE a large circle of friends all around the world. My goodness! Where everyone GO?

SIMPLE PAST	PRESENT PERFECT

1.

We use the **simple past** for a single finished action in the past. The sentence or context often includes such time clues as *yesterday*, *last week*, *last year*, or *at 2:30*. These words are not always in the sentence, but they are in the mind of the speaker.

```
_____|‾|_____|_____
       ×
     PAST          NOW
```

Last week I *attended* a party on the royal yacht.

Did you ever *go* up to that lake? (. . . when you lived in Canada)

Note: Some people use the **simple past** instead of the **present perfect** with time adverbs.

I *didn't* see them <u>yet</u>.
I <u>already</u> *saw* that movie.

This use is less formal and more conversational.

We use the **present perfect** for a past action when the time of the action isn't known or isn't important. The meaning of the tense in this case is "some time (or any time) *before now*."

```
_____?_____|_____
                   NOW
```

We often use the **present perfect** with these words:

<u>ever</u> = "at any time in your/his/her (and so on) life" in questions and negative statements.

Have you ever *gone* up to that lake?

He *hasn't* ever *been* on a yacht.

<u>never</u> = "not ever."

She's never *liked* fishing.

<u>yet</u> = "before now" in questions when the activity is expected to have happened. *Yet* is also used in negative statements.

Has she *bought* a house yet?
I *haven't seen* all the rooms yet.

<u>still</u> = "before now" in negative statements. *Still* implies that the activity should have occurred but hasn't.

She still *hasn't seen* all the rooms.

<u>already</u> = "before now" in affirmative statements and in questions. The use of *already* suggests that the activity has happened earlier than expected.

Has she already *gotten* bored?

SIMPLE PAST	PRESENT PERFECT

2. The **simple past** can also express a repeated past action. The period of time in which the action happened is also over.

NOW

They *went* there several times last year.

The **simple past** is used with phrases such as *this weekend* and *this year* if, in the speaker's mind, the time is finished. In December, a person uses the **past** with *this year* because in his or her mind the year is finished.

I *went* there twice this year.

The **present perfect** expresses one action (or the repetition of an action) that is finished. However, the period of time in which it happened is not over.

NOW

They*'ve gone* there several times this year.

This unfinished period of time may be *this week* (*weekend, month, year*), *today*, or others. Sometimes this period of time is quite long: *in the past ten years*, *in my life*, and so on. The indication of time (*this year* and so on) is not always in the sentence; it is often only in the mind of the speaker/writer.

I*'ve been* there twice (in my life).

3. The **simple past** is also used for a finished activity of some duration. (It's possible to use the word *for* with the **simple past**.)

NOW

Our family *owned* that lake <u>for</u> generations. (We don't own it now.)

The **present perfect** is used for an action happening now when we have some idea of when the action began or how long it has gone on.

NOW

Our family *has owned* that lake <u>for</u> generations. (We own it now.)

For more on this use of the **present perfect**, see Chapter 2.

4. The **simple past** is used with certain verbs to express the *beginning* of an action.

Some of these verbs are:

find out ——————————➤ know
meet —————————————➤ know
get (become) ——————————➤ be

The **present perfect** is used with certain other verbs to express the duration or continuation of an activity that was begun in the past.

Some of these verbs are:

SIMPLE PAST	PRESENT PERFECT
get (receive, buy, obtain) ⟶	➤ have
go to bed ⟶	➤ sleep
learn ⟶	➤ know
put on ⟶	➤ wear
pick up ⟶	➤ hold
catch (a cold) ⟶	➤ have (a cold)
join (a club) ⟶	➤ belong to (a club)
He *put on* that cap this morning. ⟶	➤ He*'s worn* that cap all day.
I *learned* how to drive when I was a ⟶ teenager.	➤ I*'ve known* how to drive since I was a teenager.
She *caught* a cold last week. ⟶	➤ She*'s had* a cold for a week.
They *got* married in 1980. ⟶	➤ They*'ve been* married a long time.

5.   Both the **simple past** and the **present perfect** are used with a very recently completed action, but the **present perfect** is more common.

I just *finished.*
They *bought* a lot of land recently.

I*'ve* just *finished.*
They*'ve bought* a lot of land recently.

Rap It Up

A. Oral Practice. Work with a partner. Ask and answer questions about the people in the pictures. For each of the items below the pictures ask two questions (with <u>ever</u>/<u>yet</u>). Use the time expression in the answer.

<u>**Examples:**</u>   **A:** Has she ever flown a plane?   **A:** Has she flown a plane yet?
                      B: Yes, she flew one last year.   **B:** Yes, she flew one last year.

Regina   they

1. fly a plane/last year
2. attend a party/last week
3. buy a string of pearls/last February
4. swim across the English Channel/ many years ago
5. drive a sports car/never

6. jog/yesterday
7. spend time in Acapulco/in 1996
8. lie on the Riviera/never
9. lend money to someone/in July
10. ride a camel/never

B. Work with a partner. Ask and answer questions about Oscar and Regina. Begin each question with *How often . . .* ? Use the cue words below.

Examples:

A: How often did she go to Europe last year?
B: She didn't go to Europe at all.

A: How often has she gone to Europe this year?
B: She's gone twice (two times).

			last year	this year
1.	(she)	go to Europe	0	2 times
2.	(they)	climb Mt. Fuji	1 time	0
3.	(he)	take a cruise	2 times	5 times
4.	(they)	buy some property	0	1 time

			last month	this month
5.	(he)	go fishing	2 times	0
6.	(they)	eat out	27 times	28 times
7.	(she)	throw a party	0	7 times
8.	(she)	drive Oscar crazy	15 times	2 times

			last week	this week
9.	(he)	sleep late	1 time	0
10.	(she)	forget her car keys	0	3 times

C. Work with a partner. Ask and answer questions about Regina and Oscar using the chart below.

Examples:

A: When did she buy a car?
B: She bought one in 1995.
A: Does she still own the car?
B: Yes, she's owned it since 1995.

A: When did they buy a boat?
B: They bought one in 1990.
A: Do they still own the boat?
B: No, they owned it for 5 years, but they don't anymore.

Regina   Oscar

1990	1995	last year	now
	buy a car		own a car
buy a boat ....own a boat			
join a yacht club...			belong to a yacht club
borrow money..	owe money		
	find out our address		know our address
	get sick ....get well		
become a doctor			be a doctor
buy a house	own a house		
	get married...		be married

Rap in the Real World

Conversation. Work with a partner. Ask your partner as many questions as possible using the pictures below and a time expression from the list. Use the **simple past** or **present perfect** tense.

<u>Examples:</u>

    A: Have you been in a car crash this year?
    B: No, I haven't.

    A: Were you in a car crash last year?
    B: No, I wasn't.

Time Expressions		
ever	in 1994	today
last month	4 years ago	yet
this year	in the past week	already
May	never	just

Picture Puzzle

Tenses in Context. On another piece of paper, write out the following story, changing all of the pictures and symbols to words. The characters are Oscar and Regina. Use pronouns whenever possible. If you can't guess the meaning of a symbol, check page 164 in the Appendix.

Oscar is a rich man, but he has a lot of problems. What are some of them?

The Cause of Oscar's Ulcer

〔〕'S WIFE, REGINA, (DRIVE) 〔〕 CRAZY FOR YEARS. 🗓 THEIR WEDDING ☀, 〔〕〔〕

(SWEAR) → STICK TOGETHER FOREVER, BUT THE ROMANCE (DIE) SOON AFTER THE HONEY-

MOON.

〔〕 (ALWAYS BE) RICH, BUT 〔〕 (NEVER BE) INTERESTED ☒ HIS 💵. 〔〕 (ALWAYS WANT)

A SIMPLE LIFE. BEFORE [he] (GET) MARRIED, [he] (LIKE) → GO CAMPING. [he] OFTEN (GO) HIKING ↑ ☒ THE [mountain]s. [he] (SIT) ☐☒ A STREAM ☒ THE SHADE OF A BIG [tree] OR (LIE) ☒ A HAMMOCK FOR HOURS. [calendar] WEEK ENDS, [he] (LIKE) → STAY [house] & MOW THE LAWN.

HOWEVER. [he]'S LIFE (BE) VERY DIFFERENT SINCE HIS MARRIAGE. [he] & [she] (GO) [calendar] FOUR CRUISES [boat] THE [globe] ☒ THE PAST FIVE YEARS. [she] (INSIST) [calendar] [he] BUYING [her] SO MUCH [jewelry] THAT LAST APRIL [he] (GIVE) ↑ & (BUY) [her] A [diamond] MINE. [she] (WITHDRAW) ⅓ OF THE [money] ☒ THEIR BANK ACCOUNT LAST YEAR, & [she] (WITHDRAW) ANOTHER ⅓ THIS YEAR.

RECENTLY, THE SITUATION (GET) EVEN WORSE. LAST MONTH, [she] (TEAR) ↑ THE LAWN ☒ THE BACKYARD & (TEAR) ↓ [he]'S HAMMOCK. AFTER THAT, [she] (THROW) [out] HIS FAVORITE [fish]ING [fishing rod], HIKING [boot]S, & [tent].

[he] (HAVE) AN ULCER FOR YEARS. HIS DOCTOR (OFTEN TELL) [he] → TAKE IT EASY & → STOP [drink]ING & [drink]ING. BUT [he] & [she] (JUST RECENTLY FIND) A SOLUTION → BOTH [he]'S ULCER & THEIR MARRIAGE PROBLEMS. LAST WEEK, [she] (AGREE) → GO [fish]ING W/ [he] ↑ ☒ THE [mountain]S. ☒ RETURN, [he] (AGREE) → BUY [she] A MINK [tent]. [he] [she] (GO) [calendar] THEIR [fish]ING TRIP & (HAVE) A GREAT TIME. [he] [she] (A̶R̶G̶U̶E̶) ABOUT ANYTHING SINCE THEN.

6

PAST CONTINUOUS
SIMPLE PAST

Read the story on the left. When you finish, go back to the beginning, cover up the story on the left, and choose the correct tense for each capitalized simple form of the verb to the right of the picture.

A STRANGE DAY

—This is Douglas Jones, WBC News. I'm talking to little Ginny Lee, who has an amazing story to tell. Ginny, can you tell us what *happened* yesterday afternoon?

—This is Douglas Jones, WBC News. I'm talking to little Ginny Lee, who has an amazing story to tell. Ginny, can you tell us what HAPPEN yesterday afternoon?

—We *were having* a normal Sunday afternoon when something unbelievable *happened*.

—We HAVE a normal Sunday afternoon when something unbelievable HAPPEN.

Dad *was mowing* the lawn while Mom *was fixing* the car.

Dad MOW the lawn while Mom FIX the car.

My sister, Lucy, *was peeling* potatoes and *making* a salad.

My sister, Lucy, PEEL potatoes and MAKE a salad.

My brother, Harold, *was sleeping* in the shade of the big oak tree that afternoon.

My younger sister, Sally, and her friend *were playing* ball when the commotion *began*.

I *was trying* to teach my dog, Rusty, how to shake hands (without much success) when he *began* to growl.

Even the cat, Jasmine, who *was licking* her paws, suddenly *stopped*.

I *was trying* to figure out what *was happening* when a strange object *came* down from the sky.

It *floated* down and *landed* right in our backyard while we *were* all *standing* there watching.

My brother, Harold, SLEEP in the shade of the big oak tree that afternoon.

My younger sister, Sally, and her friend PLAY ball when the commotion BEGIN.

I TRY to teach my dog, Rusty, how to shake hands (without much success) when he BEGIN to growl.

Even the cat, Jasmine, who LICK her paws, suddenly STOP.

I TRY to figure out what HAPPEN when a strange object COME down from the sky.

It FLOAT down and LAND right in our backyard while we all STAND there watching.

At first everyone *was* too afraid to move. Then we slowly *approached* the object.

We *were standing* around the object, hardly breathing, when suddenly a door *opened*.

When the door *opened*, we all *took* a step back.

Everyone *was waiting* anxiously when two little green creatures *came* out of the door.

When one of the creatures *raised* its hands, Sally *fainted*. Her friend *screamed* and *ran* into the house.

My knees *were shaking* when the creatures *stepped* onto the lawn.

At first everyone BE too afraid to move. Then we slowly APPROACH the object.

We STAND around the object, hardly breathing, when suddenly a door OPEN.

When the door OPEN, we all TAKE a step back.

Everyone WAIT anxiously when two little green creatures COME out of the door.

When one of the creatures RAISE its hands, Sally FAINT. Her friend SCREAM and RUN into the house.

My knees SHAKE when the creatures STEP onto the lawn.

Harold *was* still *sleeping* under the tree.

The two creatures *were looking* us *over* when suddenly Rusty *ran* out from under Harold's hammock.

When Rusty *saw* the creatures, he *started* to bark.

When the creatures *heard* . . .

—Oh, there you are, Ginny! I *was looking* for you. Come home now. It's time for dinner. You *weren't making up* space stories again, were you?

THE END

Harold still SLEEP under the tree.

The two creatures LOOK us OVER when suddenly Rusty RUN out from under Harold's hammock.

When Rusty SEE the creatures, he START to bark.

When the creatures HEAR . . .

—Oh, there you are, Ginny! I LOOK for you. Come home now. It's time for dinner. You NOT MAKE UP space stories again, were you?

PAST CONTINUOUS	SIMPLE PAST
1. The **past continuous** is used for an action in progress at a specific time in the past.	See Chapter 5 for several uses of the **simple past**.

1.

My brother *was sleeping* at 2:00 yesterday afternoon. (He went to sleep sometime before 2:00 and continued sleeping after 2:00.)

2.

The **past continuous** is used for a past action that was in progress when another action happened. The verb in the **past continuous** may stop when the second action occurs, or it may continue beyond the second action.

We *were having* a normal Sunday afternoon when something unbelievable happened. (We stopped having a normal afternoon.)

My knees *were shaking* when the creatures stepped onto the lawn. (My knees continued shaking.)

Note that the **past continuous** is not an independent tense. It is used with *another time* in either the sentence or context.

The **simple past** is used for the action that interrupts (or happens during) the **past continuous** action. When the **simple past** and **past continuous** are in the same sentence, the **simple past** is usually the shorter action.

When both actions are in the **simple past**, the meaning is not the same as it is when one tense is **past continuous**.

We *were eating* when he got here. (He got here during our dinner.)

We *ate* when he got here. (He got here, and then we ate.)

3.

When two actions in the past happen at the same time and we emphasize the duration of each action, we use the **past continuous** for both.

Dad *was mowing* the lawn while Mom *was fixing* the car.

PAST CONTINUOUS	SIMPLE PAST
4. The **past continuous** is often used in clauses with *while* and *as*. Dad *was mowing* the lawn while Mom *was fixing* the car. (no comma) While Dad *was mowing* the lawn, Mom *was fixing* the car. (comma) *While* and *as* both mean *when* in a continuous sense. They are usually used before a continuous tense. But sometimes the **past continuous** is used after *when*.	After *when*, the verb is usually in a simple tense such as the **simple past**. We were all standing around the object when suddenly a door *opened*. The **simple past** can also be used after *while* and *as*. When it is, the meaning is continuous. While we *watched* in horror, the strange object landed.
5. The **past continuous** is not used with verbs that have NON-ACTION meanings. (See pages 9–11.)	The **simple past** is used for NON-ACTION verbs even when the meaning is of some duration. (See pages 9–11.)
6. The **past continuous** sometimes expresses repetition in the past. I *was coughing* all night long. When the past continuous is used with *always*, *forever*, or *constantly*, it expresses a frequent activity in the past about which we feel some emotion (irritation, amusement, admiration, and so on). We *were* forever *getting* into trouble. He *was* always *asking* questions.	The **simple past** can also express repetition in the past. I *coughed* all night long. *Always* is used with the **simple past** for habitual actions in the past. I always *got up* at 6:00 when I was in high school. It is also used for a past condition. She always *liked* animals.
7. We use the **past continuous** in indirect speech when the direct quote is in the **present continuous**. "My brother *is talking* to a reporter," she said. = She said her brother *was talking* to a reporter.	We use the **simple past** in indirect speech when the direct quote is in the **simple present**. "He often *talks* to reporters," she said. = She said he often *talked* to reporters.

Rap It Up

Oral Practice. Work with a partner. Make up as many logical sentences as you can using combinations of any two of the pictures below. Use the **simple past** and the **past continuous** tenses.

Examples: I *was using* the computer while Mom *was fixing* dinner.
     Mom *was fixing* dinner when the phone *rang*.

| jog | break out | fish | blow/snow | dig |

| crash | ring | swing | fix dinner |

| sail | strike | play | chase |

| knock | lie (in a hammock) | wake up | rise |

| mow | fall | lick | use |

Rap in the Real World

A. Practice. Work with a partner. Ask your partner, "What was I doing?" at the following times:

     8:00 A.M.   10:00 A.M.   12:30 P.M.   2:00 P.M.   7:00 P.M.

Example: **A:** What was I doing at 8:00 A.M.? Guess.
     B: Were you sleeping?
     A: No.
     B: Were you eating breakfast? (Continue)

Exchange roles and repeat the exercise.

B. Conversation. Tell about an unusual event in your life. Describe what you and others were doing at the time and what happened. Examples of events: a traffic accident, an earthquake, a fire, and so on.

Fill It In

Tenses in Context. Fill in the blanks in the following story with the **simple past** or **past continuous**. Remember that more than one tense may be possible in some of the blanks.

A Strange Day on Planet Zenon

This is XR 101, Planet Zenon News. I'm talking to little TQ005 who has an amazing story to tell. TQ, can you tell us what (1)_____ (happen) yesterday?

We (2)_____ (have) a normal Sunday afternoon when something unbelievable (3)_____ (happen). Dad (4)_____ (dig) craters in the backyard while Mom (5)_____ (punch) our dinner order into the computer. My sister, RQ005, (6)_____ (check) the computer printout to make sure it (7)_____ (match) what Mom (8)_____ (order). My brother, PQ005, (9)_____ (repair) his rocket. My younger sister, VQ005, and her friend (10)_____ (do) experiments in her laboratory when the trouble (11)_____ (begin).

I (12)_____ (oil) my robot when suddenly it (13)_____ (sound) its warning alarm. When the alarm (14)_____ (begin) to ring, everyone (15)_____ (stop) what they (16)_____ (do). We (17)_____ (try) to find out why the alarm (18)_____ (ring) when a strange object (19)_____ (appear) in the sky. It (20)_____ (seem) to be coming directly toward us. And in a few minutes, it (21)_____ (land) right in Dad's newly made crater. We all (22)_____ (hold) our breath. While we (23)_____ (watch), one of the doors slowly (24)_____ (open). Then two of the ugliest creatures I've ever seen (25)_____ (step) into the doorway. I (26)_____ (hide) my eyes from the horrible sight when they (27)_____ (begin) coming closer. The robot (28)_____ (begin) to examine them as they (29)_____ (approach). When the robot's arm (30)_____ (reach) out to grab them, the two creatures (31)_____ (run) back into their ship and (32)_____ (begin) to take off again. As the ship (33)_____ (climb) back up to the sky, I (34)_____ (see) the strange markings on the side that (35)_____ (look) like this: "Planet Earth."

FUTURE IN THE PAST
SIMPLE PAST

Read the story on the left. When you finish, go back to the beginning, cover up the story on the left, and choose the correct tense for each capitalized simple form of the verb to the right of the picture.

ROCK STAR BLUES

When I *was* young, I used to dream about my future.

When I BE young, I used to dream about my future.

I *dreamed* that I *was going to be* a famous rock star.

I DREAM that I BE a famous rock star.

I *thought* people *were going to chase* me down the street, begging me for my autograph.

I THINK people CHASE me down the street, begging me for my autograph.

I *thought* that everyone *would know* me and that I *would wear* sunglasses to hide.

I THINK that everyone KNOW me and that I WEAR sunglasses to hide.

Because I *was going to be* rich, I *knew* I *was going to have* a big, beautiful house with a huge swimming pool.

I *dreamed* I *would be able* to jet to Paris for lunch.

I *thought* that I *was going to spend* my summers lying on a beach on the French Riviera.

Kings and queens *would become* my friends.

Thousands of rich, beautiful women *would beg* me to marry them.

But I always *told* myself that I *was going to be* kind and generous to those people not as lucky as I was.

Because I BE rich, I KNOW I HAVE a big, beautiful house with a huge swimming pool.

I DREAM I BE ABLE to jet to Paris for lunch.

I THINK that I SPEND my summers lying on a beach on the French Riviera.

Kings and queens BECOME my friends.

Thousands of rich, beautiful women BEG me to marry them.

But I always TELL myself that I BE kind and generous to those people not as lucky as I was.

I *knew* everyone *was going to love* my concerts.

I KNOW everyone LOVE my concerts.

Unfortunately, nobody *hired* me to give concerts.

Unfortunately, nobody HIRE me to give concerts.

I *realized* I *was* probably never *going to become* a rock star. I *decided* to become a street musician.

I REALIZE I probably never BECOME a rock star. I DECIDE to become a street musician.

No one *knew* me, and only dogs *chased* me down the street.

No one KNOW me, and only dogs CHASE me down the street.

My home *was* a bench in the park, and the only pools *were* made by the rain.

My home BE a bench in the park, and the only pools BE made by the rain.

Sometimes I *got away* for lunch, but I never *went* far.

Sometimes I GET AWAY for lunch, but I never GO far.

I *spent* my summers trying to keep cool.

I SPEND my summers trying to keep cool.

My friends *were* not kings and queens.

My friends BE not kings and queens.

Women hardly *noticed* me.

Women hardly NOTICE me.

But I still *tried* to help others as much as I could.

But I still TRY to help others as much as I could.

I *was* not famous, but to my friends, I *was* a great star.

I BE not famous, but to my friends, I BE a great star.

THE END

FUTURE IN THE PAST	SIMPLE PAST
1. The *was/were going to* form is also used in noun clauses that are the direct object of a **past tense** verb. In this way, it expresses an action that we thought (said, dreamed, and so on) would happen at some time *after* the time we thought it.	A **simple past** verb from one of the following two groups occurs before a noun clause with *would* (*verb*) or *was/were going to* (*verb*).

NOW

dreamed   was going to become (At some time "future from" the time I dreamed.)

I dreamed (that) I *was going to become* a famous rock star.

In this use, *was/were going to* (*become*) has the same meaning as *would* (*become*).

I dreamed (that) I *would become* a famous rock star.

In these clauses, the word *that* is optional.

Verbs of mental activity include:

believed	hoped
decided	imagined
doubted	knew
dreamed	predicted
felt	pretended
found out	realized
forgot	remembered
guessed	thought
had no idea	was/were sure

and

Verbs of indirect speech include:

announced	reported
boasted	said
complained	told (someone)
explained	swore
mentioned	

I *knew* (that) I was going to have a big house with a pool.

I always *said* (that) I would be kind and generous to everyone.

2. The **future in the past** is used for an action that was intended but never happened.

I *was going to become* a rock star, but I didn't know the right people in the music business.

In this use of the **future in the past**, the **simple past** is used for the reason *why* the intended action didn't happen.

I was going to become a rock star, but I *didn't know* the right people.

Rap It Up

A. Oral Practice. Column 1 below is a list of activities that Frankie and his brother wanted to do. Column 2 gives reasons why they never did them. Make as many sentences as possible combining an item from Column 1 with one from Column 2. Many combinations are possible, but make sure they are logical.

Examples: They were going to go fishing, but the car broke down.
They were going to go fishing, but they were too tired.

Column 1	Column 2
go to the movies	can't sing
call home	forget
go on a picnic	it be too hot
take photographs	be too afraid
mow the lawn	not have a car/fishing pole/film/and so on
become artists	get sick
buy their mother earrings	not have enough money
go fishing	have to take care of their baby sister
go mountain climbing	it rain
become famous singers	be too tired
go to the circus	lawn mower break/car break down/and so on
buy a newspaper	decide not to
play chess	lose crayons
go shark hunting	
join the school chorus	
make posters	

B. Work with a partner. Make up as many sentences as you can about the following pictures. Use the **simple past** and the **future in the past**.

Example: When Ginny was a child, she thought she was going to become a doctor.

Ginny
(as a child)

Rodney
(as a teenager)

Rap in the Real World

Conversation. Work with a partner. Tell about things you expected or intended that turned out differently. Make up at least 10 sentences using the **simple past** and the **future in the past**.

Examples: Before I came to this country, I thought all the cities were going to be large.
I was going to call you, but I forgot.

Picture Puzzle

Tenses in Context. On another piece of paper, write out the following story, changing all of the pictures and symbols to words. The character's name is Frankie, but you should use pronouns (he, him) whenever possible. For each of the circled verbs, choose the **past tense** or the **future in the past**. Both forms of the **future in the past** are possible in many cases. If you can't guess the meaning of a symbol, check page 164 in the Appendix.

A Day in the Life of a Street Musician

(WAKE) ↑ 1 ☼ LAST YEAR & (DECIDE) THAT IT (BE) A GOOD DAY FOR 🎸. 🖐 (PICK) ↑
HIS 🎸 & (GO) → HIS USUAL PLACE ⊠ THE 🌳. 🖐 (PUT) ↓ HIS 🎸 CASE & (BEGIN) → PLAY.
🖐 (BE) SURE A LOT OF 👥 (COME) → LISTEN → 🖐 PLAY.

AT **1**ST, THE 🌳 (BE) VERY QUIET. THERE (BE) ONLY A FEW 🐿 s & 🐦 s WHO (COME)
⊟→ BECAUSE THEY (THINK) 🖐 (GIVE) THEM SOMETHING → EAT. THEN A LOT OF 👥
(BEGIN) → RUSH ⊟→ 🖐 🕐 THEIR WAY → WORK, BUT 🖐 (KNOW) THEY (~~PUT~~) ANY 💵
⊠ HIS 🎸 CASE BECAUSE 👥 (BE) ⊠ A HURRY.

🖐 (PLAY) ALL A.M. & (THINK) ABOUT HIS FUTURE. 🖐 (KNOW) THAT 🖐 (~~BECOME~~) A
FAMOUS 🎤 ⊠ THE FUTURE. 🖐 (REALIZE) THAT 🖐 (NEVER HAVE) A BIG 🏠 W/ A
🌊ING 🏊. 🖐 (KNOW) THAT HE (NEVER BE ABLE) → BUY AN $↑ 🚗.
🖐 (BE SURE) THAT 🖐 (NEVER TRAVEL) (□↑) THE 🌍 🕐 A 🚢. 🖐 (BEGIN) → FEEL
REALLY ☹.

AT ABOUT 🕐, A POLICEWOMAN (COME) ⊟→. FOR A MINUTE, 🖐 (BE) AFRAID THAT
SHE (ARREST) 🖐 (OR AT LEAST (CHASE) 🖐 OUT OF THE 🌳) FOR PLAYING W/OUT A
PERMIT. BUT THE POLICEWOMAN JUST (STOP), (SIT) ↓ 🕐 A 🪑, & (LISTEN) → 🖐.
AFTER A FEW MINUTES, SHE (GET) ↑, (PUT) SOME 💵 ⊠ 🖐'S 🎸 CASE, & (SAY),
"YOU PLAY VERY WELL!"

THEN THE POLICEWOMAN (TELL) 🖐 THAT SHE (HAVE) A BROTHER WHO (WORK) FOR A [radio] STATION [in] ANOTHER CITY. SHE (SAY) SHE (TALK) W/ HIM [on] THE [telephone] LATER THAT

[sun] & THAT SHE (ASK) HER BROTHER → HAVE [him] PLAY HIS [guitar] [on] HIS [radio] PROGRAM.

WELL, OF COURSE [he] (BE) THRILLED. [He] (BEGIN) → DREAM THAT MAYBE [he] REALLY

(BECOME) A FAMOUS [musician]. MAYBE [he] (BE ABLE) → BUY A BIG [house] & AN [$↑] [car].

MAYBE [he] (TRAVEL) ([→]) THE [world] [on] A [ship]. MAYBE...

Fill in the blanks with the following tenses. In some cases, more than one tense may be possible.

Simple Past

Present Perfect

Past Continuous

Future in the Past (*would* or *be going to* + simple form)

Great-Aunt Bertha vs. the City Council

My Great-Aunt Bertha is 95 years old, and she lives alone in a big old house on Kingsley Drive, where she (1)_____ (live) for over sixty years. In the past decade, we (2)_____ (try) many times to persuade her to move in with us, but she's a very cranky, stubborn lady; she (3)_____ (be) quite independent all her life, so she's quite happy living there with only her five dogs for company.

Well, last month the city council (4)_____ (decide) that they (5)_____ (build) a parking lot on her property. They (6)_____ (send) an eviction notice saying that they (7)_____ (buy) her house and tear it down, so she (8)_____ (have to) move. Aunt Bertha was absolutely furious. She (9)_____ (tell) them that she (10)_____ (not move) anywhere.

The Great Battle (11)_____ (begin).

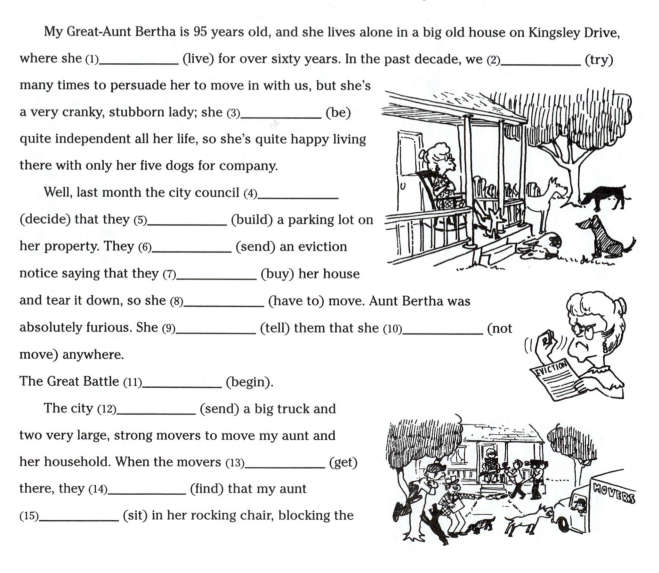

The city (12)_____ (send) a big truck and two very large, strong movers to move my aunt and her household. When the movers (13)_____ (get) there, they (14)_____ (find) that my aunt (15)_____ (sit) in her rocking chair, blocking the front door. They (16)_____ (wonder) what to do when her five dogs (17)_____ (appear) and (18)_____ (chase) them off.

   While the movers (19)_____ (scream) and (20)_____ (run) around the yard, some reporters (21)_____ (arrive) from the local newspaper and from WTTV news. The reporters (22)_____ (take) one look around and (23)_____ (start) to laugh. One of the movers (24)_____ (hide) in his truck as one of the dogs (25)_____ (make) sure that he stayed there. The other mover, up in an elm tree,

(26)_____ (cling) to one of the branches while a second dog (27)_____ (growl) at him from below. The reporters (28)_____ (sit) down and (29)_____ (ask) Aunt Bertha what in the world (30)_____ (happen).

   That night Aunt Bertha (31)_____ (appear) on the evening news and in the *Daily Herald*. She soon (32)_____ (become) famous. The people of the city (33)_____ (be) quite angry with the city council. The council members finally (34)_____ (decide) that they (35)_____ (not build) the parking lot on my aunt's property, after all. My aunt (36)_____ (be) so happy about this news that she (37)_____ (throw) a huge party and invited everyone—even the movers and the city council!

   Aunt Bertha (38)_____ (be) very pleased ever since then, and we (39)_____ (notice) a change in her. She (40)_____ (become) less cranky!

Finish the Story

Use the phrases and pictures on this page to help you rewrite the story of Great-Aunt Bertha. **Do not look back at the original story**. Your story won't be exactly the same as the original, but you should correctly use the four tenses from this unit. The verbs on this page are in either picture form or the simple form, but you will choose from the following tenses when you rewrite the story on the next page: **simple past**, **present perfect**, **past continuous**, and **future in the past** (*was/were going to* or *would*).

Cue Sheet

1. live for sixty years
   try to persuade her to move
   be cranky, stubborn
   be independent (all her life)

2. city council—decide/build
   send an eviction notice
   buy/tear down her house
   have to move
   tell them/not move
   Great Battle/begin

3. city—send a big truck
   movers—find my aunt
   wonder
   five dogs—appear/chase
   movers—scream/run
   reporters—arrive/take
   movers—hide/cling
   dog—growl
   reporters—sit down/ask

4. Aunt Bertha—appear
   become famous
   people—be angry
   city council—decide/not build
   aunt—be happy/throw a party

5. be pleased since then
   we—notice a change
   she—become

Great-Aunt Bertha vs. the City Council

My Aunt Bertha is very old. She lives alone on Kingsley Drive, where she . . .

Story Line

A. Use this Story Line to answer the questions on the next page. The verbs on this page are in the past tense, but you'll choose the correct tenses.

Aunt Bertha's Life

1900

- Bertha was born
- Family lived on a farm in Vermont

1909

- Decided to become a dancer
- Her parents planned for her to become a farmer's wife

1918

- Graduated from high school (June 2)
- Got on a train to San Francisco (June 3)
- Met Julian (a farmer) on the train

- Began dance lessons (nights)
- Julian bought a farm outside San Francisco

1919

- Julian proposed marriage
- Bertha said "no"

1921

- She tried to get a job as a dancer
- All of the theaters said "no"

1922

- Julian sold the farm
- Julian proposed marriage
- Bertha said "yes"

- They moved to Los Angeles
- Julian bought a shop

1923

- Bertha began giving dance lessons
- She broke her arm during a dance lesson

1930

- They bought a house on Kingsley Drive
- Bertha planned to open her own dance school in 1931
- Had a baby girl

1931

- Had a baby boy
- Didn't open a dance school
- Planned for her daughter to become a dancer

1943

- Her daughter graduated from high school
- Her daughter got on a train to New York
- Her daughter became a dancer

1951

- Bertha bought a dance studio and hired dance teachers

1970

- Julian died of a heart attack while on a plane to New York
- Bertha refused ever to get on a plane

Now

- Still lives on Kingsley Drive
- Goes to the ballet often

B. Look at the Story Line on the previous page and answer these questions. Be sure to use the same tenses as in the questions.

1. Where was Bertha's family living when she was born?
2. In 1909, what did she decide she was going to become?
3. What did her parents think she was going to become?
4. Where was she going when she met Julian?
5. Why do you think she said "no" to Julian's proposal?
6. What was she going to become?
7. Why did she change her mind and accept his proposal?
8. What was Bertha doing when she broke her arm?
9. What did she hope her daughter would become when she grew up?
10. What was Julian doing when he died?
11. How long has she lived on Kingsley Drive?
12. How many cities has she lived in?
13. How long has she been interested in dancing?
14. How many houses has she owned?
15. Has she ever ridden on a train?
16. Has she ever flown on an airplane?

It's Your Turn. Practice the **simple past**, **present perfect**, **past continuous**, and **future in the past** (*was/were going to* or *would*) in the following exercises.

A. Draw a story line with major events in your own life or the life of someone in your family. It probably won't have as many events as Bertha's has, but you should try to have as many events and plans as possible.

B. Briefly tell another student about your story line. Then exchange your story line with another student's. Ask and answer questions about the details of each other's lives, using the story line as a basis.

Examples:

A: Why did your parents hope you would become a doctor?
B: Doctors are respected a lot in my country.
A: Why did you want to become a journalist?
B: I've always been interested in writing and in traveling. I thought I'd be able to do both as a journalist.

A: What part of Hong Kong were you living in when you started school?
B: We were living in Kowloon, near the railroad.
A: How did you get to school each day?
B: I walked. Sometimes I took the bus.

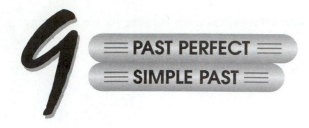

Read the story on the left. When you finish, go back to the beginning, cover up the story on the left, and choose the correct tense for each capitalized simple form of the verb to the right of the picture.

A SATURDAY HIKE

Sam and Charlie *decided* to go on a hike last Saturday.

Sam and Charlie DECIDE to go on a hike last Saturday.

Sam *drove* over and *picked up* Charlie because Charlie's car *had broken down*.

Sam DRIVE over and PICK UP Charlie because Charlie's car BREAK DOWN.

Sam *had gotten* his driver's license only two weeks earlier, so he *was* a little nervous.

Sam GET his driver's license only two weeks earlier, so he BE a little nervous.

But they finally *got* to the mountains.

But they finally GET to the mountains.

Charlie *said* that he *had found* a beautiful trail a few weeks earlier.

Charlie SAY that he FIND a beautiful trail a few weeks earlier.

He *had followed* it up to a lake . . .

He FOLLOW it up to a lake . . .

. . . but he *didn't go* swimming because of the cold water.

. . . but he NOT GO swimming because of the cold water.

So on Saturday, Charlie *led* the way.

So on Saturday, Charlie LEAD the way.

Sam *had* some trouble keeping up with him.

Sam HAVE some trouble keeping up with him.

They *got* very thirsty because they *had forgotten* to bring something to drink.

They GET very thirsty because they FORGET to bring something to drink.

Finally, they *reached* the lake and *sat* down on a rock to rest.

Finally, they REACH the lake and SIT down on a rock to rest.

Charlie *was* hungry because he *hadn't brought* his lunch.

Charlie BE hungry because he NOT BRING his lunch.

Sam *was* hungry because he *had fed* his sandwich to animals along the trail.

Sam BE hungry because he FEED his sandwich to animals along the trail.

Their feet *hurt* so much that they almost *couldn't move*.

Their feet HURT so much that they almost CANNOT MOVE.

On the way back down the mountain, they *lost* the trail.

On the way back down the mountain, they LOSE the trail.

By the time they *got* home, the sun *had set*, and it *was* dark.

By the time they GET home, the sun SET and it BE dark.

A bee *had stung* Sam . . .

. . . a snake *had bitten* Charlie . . .

. . . and both of them *had frozen* in the lake.

They *were* very glad to be home.

They both *decided* never to go hiking again.

A bee STING Sam . . .

. . . a snake BITE Charlie . . .

. . . and both of them FREEZE in the lake.

They BE very glad to be home.

They both DECIDE never to go hiking again.

THE END

PAST PERFECT	SIMPLE PAST
1. We use the **past perfect** when we speak or write in the **past tense** and then "jump back" to an earlier action. PAST PERFECT ——— PAST ——— NOW He was hungry because he *hadn't eaten* breakfast. This "jump" can be any length of time—years, months, days, or even minutes.	We usually use the **simple past** if we move *forward* in time (toward the present) and if it is clear which action happened first. In casual conversation, some people don't use the **past perfect**, even when they "jump back" in time. Instead, they use the **simple past**. He was hungry because he *didn't eat* breakfast.
2. In a story, we often jump back and forth from the **simple past** to the **past perfect**. The story at the beginning of this chapter is an illustration of this. 7:00 PAST — 9:00 A.M. NOW — beginning of the story 7:00 PAST PERFECT — 9:00 PAST — 11:00 NOW — middle 7:00 — 9:00 PAST PERFECT — 11:00 PAST — 5:00 P.M. NOW — end	
3. We often use the **past perfect** in sentences with adverbial clauses beginning with *until*, *before*, *after*, *when*, *because*, and *although*. Although Charlie *had been* there a few weeks earlier, he lost the trail on the way home. (comma)	With *before* and *after*, the **past perfect** is not always used. It isn't necessary because the time is clear. Instead, we may use the **simple past**. Sam *had grabbed* his camera before he left. (correct) Sam *grabbed* his camera before he left. (also correct)

PAST PERFECT	SIMPLE PAST
Charlie lost the trail on the way home although he *had been* there a few weeks earlier. (no comma) It's important to use the **past perfect** when *when* means *before,* in order to avoid confusion. Charlie *had packed* his lunch *when* Sam picked him up.	However, we use only the **past perfect** when *before* is the last word in the clause or sentence. Sam *had* never *used* the camera before. (= before that time)

4. We often use the **past perfect** with these words:

just
recently
already   (These adverbs
scarcely   usually come
barely   between *had*
ever   and the *past
never   participle.*)
yet
still

He *had* just *fed* his sandwich to some animals.

He *had* never *seen* a lion so close before.

Instead of meaning "before *now*" as they do with the **present perfect**, these words mean "before *then*" with the **past perfect**.

We also use the **past perfect** with *since* and *for* if we know when an activity began before another past activity, or how long it went on.

I realized that I *hadn't eaten* a single French fry since I started my diet.

Note that the **past perfect** is not an independent tense. It is used with **the past tense** in either the sentence or context.

Past Perfect	Simple Past
5. We often use the **past perfect** in noun clauses—frequently when we use indirect speech. "I found the trail," he said. = He said he *had found* the trail. "I've found the trail," he said. = He said he *had found* the trail.	
6.	When the main verb of a sentence is in the **past perfect** and the action in a relative clause occurs at the *same time*, we use the **simple past** for the verb in the relative clause. The animals had been in cages that *looked* like jail cells. **Note:** For a complete chart of tenses in relative clauses, see page 159 in the Appendix.

Fill It In

Tenses in Context. Fill in the blanks in the following story with the **simple past** or **past perfect** tense. Remember that more than one tense may be possible in some of the blanks.

An Outing

Sam and Charlie (1)_____ (go) to Lion Country Safari last weekend. They (2)_____ (never be) there before, so they (3)_____ (be) really excited.

They (4)_____ (go) to a small zoo a few months before. There, the animals (5)_____ (be) in cages that (6)_____ (look) like jail cells, and they (7)_____ (sleep) on cold, cement floors. They (8)_____ (look) miserable.

But at Lion Country Safari, the animals (9)_____ (be) almost as free to roam as they (10)_____ (be) back in Africa. They (11)_____ (eat), (12)_____ (sleep),

(13)_____ (fight), and (14)_____ (play) just as they (15)_____ (do) in Africa—in a natural environment of dirt, trees, plants, rocks, and streams.

Sam and Charlie (16)_____ (drive) slowly through the area. At one point, a camel (17)_____ (stick) his head through the car window, and Charlie, overjoyed, (18)_____ (give) him his peanut butter sandwich. Sam (19)_____ (tell) him not to do it again because feeding the animals (20)_____ (be) against regulations. A few minutes later, they (21)_____ (be) terrified when the lions (22)_____ (come) right over to the car to "visit." Sam almost (23)_____ (drive) off the road because he (24)_____ (never see) a lion so close before. Charlie (25)_____ (not get) to see the elephants because he (26)_____ (dive) onto the floor of the car in fright at the first sight of the lions.

That afternoon, on the way home, Sam (27)_____ (be) angry with himself because he (28)_____ (forget) to bring his camera, and Charlie (29)_____ (be) hungry because he (30)_____ (feed) his lunch to the camel. But, aside from that, it (31)_____ (be) a good day.

Rap It Up

Oral Practice. In Column 1 are some things that have happened to Charlie. In Column 2 are the reasons for these occurrences. Make logical sentences by combining an item from Column 1 with one from Column 2. Make as many sentences as possible in the **simple past** and the **past perfect**.

Example: Charlie lost weight because he had exercised.

Column 1	Column 2
not have money to pay for groceries	eat too much
pass his English test	go to bed late
take the bus to work	not read the directions
lose weight	go on a diet
get a promotion	lose his wallet
borrow money from Sam	forget to set his alarm
wake up late	spend all his money on candy
become overweight	exercise
ruin a cake	work hard
fail his French test	not understand the lesson
get tired	someone—steal car
be late for work	study very hard

Rap in the Real World

A. Oral Practice. Work with a partner. Using the following schedule of Sam's life, ask and answer as many logical questions as possible. Use the **simple past** and the **past perfect**. The question words in the right-hand column will help you get started.

<u>Examples:</u>

    A: Where had he worked before he returned to medical school?
    B: He'd worked in a restaurant.
    A: How many restaurants had he worked in?
    B: He'd worked in three.

Sam

	15 years ago	**5 years ago**	**last year**	**question words**
education	finish third year at Lawson Medical School drop out of Lawson	go back to Lawson	graduate from Lawson	How long ago How many times How many years Where When
career	work in restaurant after leaving school	quit third restaurant in 10 years	begin work at hospital	
travel	week's vacation in Boston	2 weeks in Boston	move to Boston	
love life	break up with fifth girlfriend in one year meet Mary Lou in Boston	propose to Mary Lou in Boston	marry Mary Lou	

B. Conversation. Make your own schedule for education, career, and so on, like the one above. Exchange schedules with your neighbor and ask each other questions using the **simple past** and the **past perfect**. You may ask questions that bring in information not on the schedule.

PAST PERFECT CONTINUOUS
PAST CONTINUOUS
SIMPLE PAST

Read the story on the left. When you finish, go back to the beginning, cover up the story on the left, and choose the correct tense for each capitalized simple form of the verb to the right of the picture.

THE SPY

—I think we should give Agent Dudley Dangerfield his old job back. He has a lot of experience. He *had been spying* for the Xenrovian government since 1990 when he *decided* to come to us.

He *had been doing a good* job for us until he *went* over to "the other side."

The queen of Xenrovia *gave* him a large sum of money when he *left*.

—I don't know, Chief. I *heard* some bad things about him while I *was checking* his employment record.

—I think we should give Agent Dudley Dangerfield his old job back. He has a lot of experience. He SPY for the Xenrovian government since 1990 when he DECIDE to come to us.

He DO a good job for us until he GO over to "the other side."

The queen of Xenrovia GIVE him a large sum of money when he LEAVE.

—I don't know, Chief. I HEAR some bad things about him while I CHECK his employment record.

I *found out* that the queen *was* only *trying* to make him leave quickly because he *had been making* so many mistakes.

For example, he *took* secret photographs of the wrong military installation although he *had been studying* the maps for three months.

Then, while he was *taking* the photographs, he almost *fell* out of the plane.

—That was probably because he *had been taking* flying lessons only since February.

—Of course, there *was* also the problem with the ambassador.

Dangerfield *had been guarding* him for about a week when the ambassador *went* for a walk in the park.

I FIND OUT that the queen only TRY to make him leave quickly because he MAKE so many mistakes.

For example, he TAKE secret photographs of the wrong military installation although he STUDY the maps for three months.

Then, while he TAKE the photographs, he almost FALL out of the plane.

—That was probably because he TAKE flying lessons only since February.

—Of course, there BE also the problem with the ambassador.

Dangerfield GUARD him for about a week when the ambassador GO for a walk in the park.

While Dangerfield *was flirting* with a girl in the park, three men *kidnapped* the ambassador.

While Dangerfield FLIRT with a girl in the park, three men KIDNAP the ambassador.

The kidnapping *caused* problems for Dangerfield, because he *had been hoping* for a salary increase.

The kidnapping CAUSE problems for Dangerfield, because he HOPE for a salary increase.

Then, as you know, he *came* to work for us.

Then, as you know, he COME to work for us.

—But why *did* we *hire* such an idiot?

—But why we HIRE such an idiot?

—Well, actually, when we hired him, we *weren't* aware of how badly he *had been doing* in Xenrovia.

—Well, actually, when we hired him, we BE NOT aware of how badly he DO in Xenrovia.

And he *was doing* surprisingly well for us until the other side *offered* him more money, a yearly ocean cruise, and a home computer.

And he DO surprisingly well for us until the other side OFFER him more money, a yearly ocean cruise, and a home computer.

He *took* their offer and *moved* there because we *hadn't been paying* him so well.

He TAKE their offer and MOVE there because we NOT PAY him so well.

But he *got* into trouble last month with his boss. He *was daydreaming* one day as he *was driving* his boss to the airport . . .

But he GET into trouble last month with his boss. He DAYDREAM one day as he DRIVE his boss to the airport . . .

. . . and he *ran into* an oak tree. His boss *flew* out of the car and *landed* in a fountain.

. . . and he RUN INTO an oak tree. His boss FLY out of the car and LAND in a fountain.

When they *fished* him out of the fountain, he *was yelling* something about punching Dudley Dangerfield from there to the middle of the Atlantic.

When they FISH him out of the fountain, he YELL something about punching Dudley Dangerfield from there to the middle of the Atlantic.

—I *was thinking* about hiring him back, but I've just changed my mind. It's good to have him on the other side.

—I THINK about hiring him back, but I've just changed my mind. It's good to have him on the other side.

THE END

PAST PERFECT CONTINUOUS	PAST CONTINUOUS

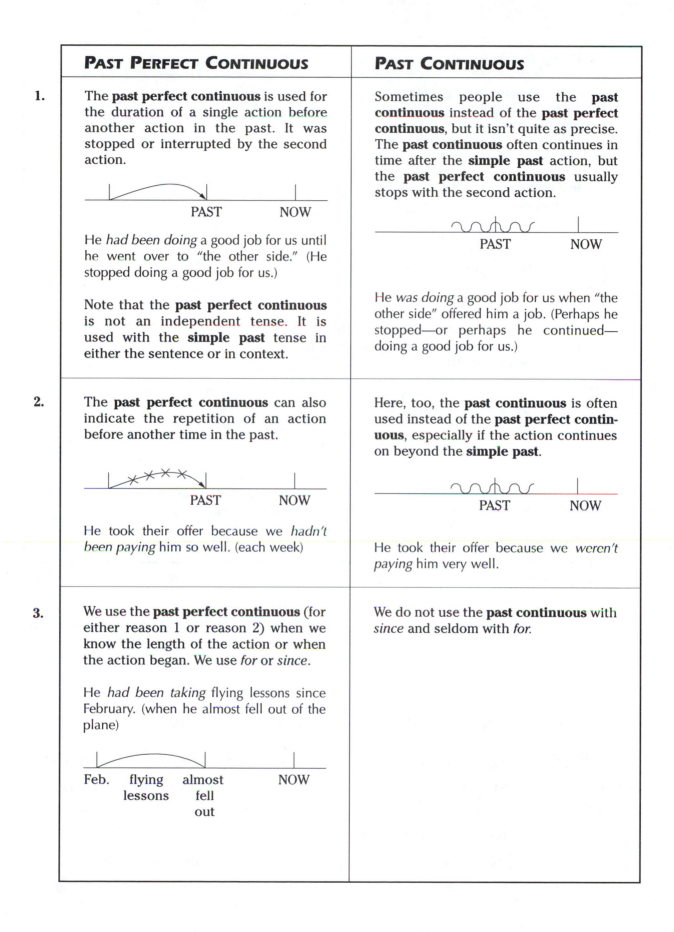

1.

PAST PERFECT CONTINUOUS

The **past perfect continuous** is used for the duration of a single action before another action in the past. It was stopped or interrupted by the second action.

PAST   NOW

He *had been doing* a good job for us until he went over to "the other side." (He stopped doing a good job for us.)

Note that the **past perfect continuous** is not an independent tense. It is used with the **simple past** tense in either the sentence or in context.

PAST CONTINUOUS

Sometimes people use the **past continuous** instead of the **past perfect continuous**, but it isn't quite as precise. The **past continuous** often continues in time after the **simple past** action, but the **past perfect continuous** usually stops with the second action.

PAST   NOW

He *was doing* a good job for us when "the other side" offered him a job. (Perhaps he stopped—or perhaps he continued—doing a good job for us.)

2.

The **past perfect continuous** can also indicate the repetition of an action before another time in the past.

PAST   NOW

He took their offer because we *hadn't been paying* him so well. (each week)

Here, too, the **past continuous** is often used instead of the **past perfect continuous**, especially if the action continues on beyond the **simple past**.

PAST   NOW

He took their offer because we *weren't paying* him very well.

3.

We use the **past perfect continuous** (for either reason 1 or reason 2) when we know the length of the action or when the action began. We use *for* or *since*.

He *had been taking* flying lessons since February. (when he almost fell out of the plane)

Feb.   flying   almost   NOW
     lessons   fell
         out

We do not use the **past continuous** with *since* and seldom with *for*.

	PAST PERFECT CONTINUOUS	PAST CONTINUOUS
4.	The **past perfect continuous** is not used with a specific amount or a specific number of times. For example, we do not use the **past perfect continuous** with such phrases as *twice, five times, 20 pounds,* or *15 thousand dollars.* Instead, we use the **past perfect** with such phrases. He said he *had been losing* a lot of weight. He said he *had lost* 20 pounds.	
5.	We use the **past perfect continuous** in indirect speech when the direct quote was in the **past continuous**. "They weren't paying him very well," she said. = She said they *hadn't been paying* him very well.	
	As with the other continuous tenses, we do not use either the **past perfect continuous** or the **past continuous** with NON-ACTION verbs. (See pages 9–11.) To check the use of the **simple past**, refer to Chapters 5, 6, 7, and 9.	

Picture Puzzle

Tenses in Context. On another piece of paper, write out the following story, changing all of the pictures and symbols to words. The character is Dudley Dangerfield (from the story earlier in this chapter), but you should use pronouns whenever possible. For each of the circled verbs, choose the **simple past**, **past continuous**, or **past perfect continuous**.

One day a few years ago, Dudley decided to take a vacation from spying. But . . .

A Day in the Life of Dudley Dangerfield

(LOOK FORWARD) → HIS VACATION FOR A LONG TIME WHEN FINALLY (GET) TO HAWAII. (WORK) VERY HARD & (NEED) → RELAX. HIS 1ST @ THE , (LAY) HIS THE & (LIE) ↓ IT. (PUT) HIS & (BEGIN) → READ A FLYING. WHILE (READ), (FALL) ASLEEP. WHEN (WAKE) ↑, (REALIZE) THAT (SLEEP) FOR THREE HOURS, & HIS 1ST (BE) ALMOST ˣ□.

HIS 2ND , (LIE) ⊠ A HAMMOCK □ˣ A WHEN (START) → THINK ABOUT HIS HEALTH. (BE) A LITTLE OVERWEIGHT BECAUSE (EAT) A LOT OF TERRIFIC INTERNATIONAL FOOD EVER SINCE

(GET) HIS **1**ST JOB AS A SPY. [🕵] (DECIDE) → GO 🍴 A DIET, SWEAT [X] THE SAUNA EVERY ☀, ¢ JOG

5 MILES EVERY [A.M.]. [🕵] (THINK) ABOUT GETTING [X] SHAPE FOR THE ANNUAL INTERNATIONAL SPY 🏓

TOURNAMENT WHEN SUDDENLY [🕵] (HEAR) A LOUD SCREAM FROM SOMEWHERE ↓ THE 〰.

[🕵] (JUMP) ↑ ¢ (RUN) ↓ THE 〰 → SEE WHAT THE COMMOTION (BE). [🕵] (SEE) A WOMAN [X] THE

〰〰 . SHE (SCREAM) ¢ (THRASH) [☐⤴] ¢ (APPEAR) → BE DROWNING. 🍴 THE 〰, A FEW 👥 (RUN)

[☐⤴] ¢ (TRY) → FIND A LIFEGUARD. [🕵] (JUMP) [X], (SWIM) [☐⤴], ¢ (PULL) HER → SHORE. SOMEONE 🍴 THE

〰 (SPREAD) A 📄 🍴 THE SAND, ¢ [🕵] (PUT) HER 🍴 IT. SOMEONE ELSE [X] THE CROWD (SAY) THAT

THE WOMAN (TRY) → SWIM → SHORE FROM A 🚢. FINALLY, THE WOMAN (OPEN) HER 👁 👁, ¢ [🕵] (SEE)

THAT SHE (BE) FINE. [🕵] ALSO (NOTICE) THAT SHE (BE) GORGEOUS. [🕵] (BEGIN) → FALL [X] LOVE W/ HER WHEN

THE POLICE (RUN) ↑ ¢ (ARREST) HER. THEY (SAY) THAT SHE (BE) AN INTERNATIONAL CRIMINAL WHO (FOLLOW)

[🕵] FOR SEVERAL WEEKS. SHE (PLAN) → KIDNAP [🕵] FOR HER GOVERNMENT SINCE THE **1**ST OF THE MONTH.

THE POLICE (TRY) → CAPTURE HER SINCE SHE (GET) → HAWAII.

THAT [P.M.], WHILE THE ☀ (SLOWLY SET), [🕵] (TAKE) A WALK ↑ THE 〰. AS [🕵] (WALK), [🕵] (THINK)

W/ REGRET ABOUT HIS WOULD-BE ROMANCE. [🕵] (CONSIDER) EXPLORING A NEW LINE OF WORK.

Rap It Up

Look at the following columns and ask a partner questions using the **past continuous** or **past perfect continuous** tense and a phrase from Column 1. To answer, your partner will use as many phrases from Column 2 as possible.

Examples: **A:** What had Dudley been doing when the computer crashed?
B: He had been doing research on the Internet.

A: What was Dudley doing when the phone rang?
B: He was feeding the cat.

Column 1	Column 2
fire break out	mow the lawn all afternoon
storm start	study maps for 3 hours
phone ring	drive a car all night
computer crash	feed the cat
tires blow out	do research on the Internet
bee sting	chase a spy

Rap in the Real World

Ask your partner questions about his/her day using "How long" and the **past perfect continuous** tense. Here is a suggestion:

Example: **A:** How long had you been sitting in class when the bell rang?
B: I'd been sitting there for 20 minutes when the bell rang.

bell ring	fall asleep	alarm go off
teacher walk into class	lesson begin	bus arrive

11 PAST TENSE REVIEW

Fill in the blanks with the following tenses. In some cases, more than one tense is possible.

Simple Past

Past Continuous

Past Perfect

Past Perfect Continuous

How I Changed My Life

I go to the Gorgeous Body Health Club four times a week. When I (1)_____ (begin) going there, I (2)_____ (be) in terrible shape. I (3)_____ (not ever go) to a health club before, and I (4)_____ (not eat) right for years. On the day I (5)_____ (join) the club, I (6)_____ (be) thirty pounds overweight, and my girlfriend (7)_____ (worry) about my health for a long time.

On the first day of my new exercise program, I (8)_____ (run) a mile, (9)_____ (swim) twenty laps, (10)_____ (take) a half-hour exercise class, and (11)_____ (sweat) in the sauna. I (12)_____ (think) I was going to die! While I (13)_____ (sweat) in the sauna, I (14)_____ (dream) about going home to an enormous sandwich, French fries, a Coke, and a huge hot fudge sundae!

But at that time, nobody (15)_____ (tell) me about the diet program at the health club. I (16)_____ (change) clothes in the locker room and (17)_____ (think) about my hot fudge sundae when my exercise instructor (18)_____ (come) up and (19)_____ (tell) me that the diet class (20)_____ (just begin) and that I (21)_____ (be) five minutes late. "Diet class?" I (22)_____ (say), horrified. I (23)_____ (tell) him that nobody (24)_____ (mention) such a thing to me.

Well, I somewhat reluctantly (25)_____ (go) over to the diet class. When I (26)_____ (walk) in, a terribly thin young woman (27)_____ (give) a lecture on all the foods we shouldn't eat. She (28)_____ (point) to a list of forbidden foods which she (29)_____ (put) on the blackboard. All my hopes (30)_____ (sink) when I (31)_____ (see) all my favorite foods

on the list. Then the young woman (32)_____ (say)

that she (33)_____ (come) to Gorgeous Body for two

years and (34)_____ (teach) the diet class for six

months. She (35)_____ (tell) us she (36)_____

(weigh) 197 pounds when she (37)_____ (start) the

program. Of course that (38)_____ (be) very inspiring!

Everyone in the class (39)_____ (swear) to come to

class regularly and to keep the strict diet.

    This (40)_____ (be) all a year ago. One day at lunchtime last week, as I (41)_____

(eat) my spinach salad, I (42)_____ (think) about how my life (43)_____ (change) and

how wonderful I (44)_____ (become). I (45)_____ (not eat) a single French fry since I

started my diet. I (46)_____ (exercise) two hours a day for the past year. And for several weeks

I (47)_____ (think) of entering the Mr. America Contest. I (48)_____ (try) many times

to persuade my girlfriend to join the health club and

become as healthy and as perfect as I was. However,

as I (49)_____ (drink) my nonfat milk, I sadly

(50)_____ (remember) that she (51)_____

(recently leave) me. She said that I (52)_____

(become) a new person but that she (53)_____

(prefer) the old me to the thin, vain one. She said it

seemed that I (54)_____ (trade in) a pleasant

personality for a Mr. America body, and she didn't

think it was a good trade.

Finish the Story

Use the phrases and pictures on this page to help you rewrite Harry's story. **Do not look back at the original story**. Your story won't be exactly the same as the original, but you should correctly use the four tenses from this unit. The verbs on this page are in either picture form or the simple form, but you will choose from the following tenses when you rewrite the story on the next page: **simple past, past continuous, past perfect,** and **past perfect continuous**. Instead of telling the story in the first person (I/my/we), use the third person (he/his/them).

Cue Sheet

1. never go before
   not eat right
   girlfriend

2.

3. nobody tell
   change clothes
   come up
   "The diet class has just begun."
   nobody mention

4. "I've been coming here for 2 years, and I've been teaching this class for 6 months. I weighed 197 pounds two years ago."

5. not eat a single French fry
   exercise 2 hours a day for a year
   think of entering Mr. America Contest
   girlfriend recently leave
   "You have become a new person, but I loved the old one."

How Harry Changed His Life

When Harry began going to the Gorgeous Body Health Club, he had never gone to a health club before, and he . . .

Story Line

Use the following Story Line to help you answer the questions on the next page. This Story Line will help you understand how Harry (the fellow at the Gorgeous Body Health Club) came to be overweight in the first place. The verbs on this page are all in the simple form. You should choose the correct tense.

Harry's Life

1967	1971	1972	1973
• Be born in New York City	• Begin nursery school • (A little kid) hit him, (nose) bleed, cling to teacher	• Begin kindergarten • Be very shy • Want a dog	• (Family) move to the suburbs • Get a dog • Start first grade • Be very shy

1974	1976	1977	1979
• Feed dog/(dog) bite Harry • Begin to be afraid of dogs • Give dog away	• Ride first horse • Begin horseback riding lessons	• Fall off horse & break arm • Begin to be afraid of horses • Quit riding	• Go camping with parents • Sleep outdoors for the first time • Swim in lake/almost drown • Begin to be scared of swimming

1982	1987	1990	1991
• Take first dancing lesson/step on his partner's foot • (She) tease him • Begin to be shy with girls • Begin to eat too much	• Be overweight • Start to look for a job	• Continue to be overweight • Continue to look for a job (June - Dec.)	• Find a job as a computer programmer • Continue to be overweight • Find a girlfriend

The year before last	Last year	
• Join "Gorgeous Body Health Club" (Dec.) • Begin to jog, swim, take exercise classes, diet	• Continue going to the club, lose 30 lbs. & all his shyness • Get a dog; go campng; begin horseback riding	• Become selfish, superficial, & overly confident • (Girlfriend) leave him • Quit health club • (Girlfriend) come back

Look at the Story Line on the previous page and answer these questions. Use the following tenses: **simple past**, **past continuous**, **past perfect**, and **past perfect continuous**.

1. Where was Harry's family living when he was born?
2. When did he begin nursery school?
3. What happened one day at nursery school? What else? Who did he cling to?
4. When he began kindergarten in 1972, had he been to school before?
5. Where did the family move in 1973? What did they get?
6. How long had Harry been having problems with shyness when he started the first grade?
7. Why did Harry begin to be afraid of dogs? What was he doing when this happened? What did they do with the dog?
8. When did he ride his first horse? Where was the family living when he began riding lessons?
9. How long had he been taking riding lessons when he decided to quit? Why did he decide to quit?
10. What happened when he went camping with his parents?
11. Why did his dance partner tease him at his first lesson?
12. What was he doing in October, 1990?
13. How long had he been looking for a job when he found the job as a computer programmer?
14. What changed his life the year before last? Why was Harry overweight at the time he joined the club?
15. Why do you think he became more confident? How did he overcome his fears and his shyness?
16. Why did his girlfriend leave him? Why did she come back?

It's Your Turn. In a group of 3–4 students, one student will make a statement about himself. (Examples: I'm shy./I'm afraid of water./I hate cats./I'm an engineer.) The other students will ask questions to find out the steps that led to this characteristic/fear/condition/job. Use the **past**, **past continuous**, **past perfect**, and **past perfect continuous**.

<u>Example:</u>   **A:** I hate cats.
　　　　　　　B: When did you first notice this?
　　　　　　　A: Well, a cat bit me when I was 12.
　　　　　　　B: Had you been around cats before that time?

Then a second student will make a statement and answer questions, and so on.

CUMULATIVE REVIEW

Fill in the blanks with the tenses we've studied so far. In some cases, more than one tense may be possible.

Simple Present	**Past Continuous**
Present Continuous	**Future in the Past** (*was/were going to* or *would*)
Present Perfect	**Past Perfect**
Present Perfect Continuous	**Past Perfect Continuous**
Simple Past	

My Two Careers

I.

One summer when I (1)_____ (be) a teenager, I (2)_____ (get) a job with the circus. As part of my job, I (3)_____ (stick) up posters all over the city, (4)_____ (set) up chairs in the tent, and (5)_____ (sell) tickets. I (6)_____ (learn) a lot about circus life that summer, and I (7)_____ (love) circuses ever since then.

Unfortunately, the circus that I (8)_____ (work) for (9)_____ (not be) a very successful one. Things (10)_____ (forever go) wrong. One night, for example, we (11)_____ (begin) the performance very late. I (12)_____ (already shut) down the box office, and everyone (13)_____ (sit) in the tent. The audience (14)_____ (already eat) all of the hot dogs and ice cream cones, and they (15)_____ (grow) restless. I (16)_____ (think) that the crowd (17)_____ (throw) tomatoes or something at the ringmaster because they (18)_____ (be) so irritated. Finally, the show (19)_____ (begin).

The ringmaster (20)_____ (lead) the parade of animals and performers into the tent. He (21)_____ (look) quite nervous because the gypsy fortune-teller who always (22)_____ (travel) with the circus (23)_____ (see) terrible things in her crystal ball all day long. She (24)_____ (warn) him for weeks not to put on this performance, and he (25)_____ (threaten) to fire her unless she (26)_____ (give) him some better predictions.

Anyway, I (27)_____ (watch) the whole show that night. Everything (28)_____ (go) fine at first. Three elephants (29)_____ (do) tricks in the center ring. In another ring, the lion tamer (30)_____ (get) one of his lions to jump through a ring of fire. The lion (31)_____ (be) very cranky all day, but she (32)_____ (do) pretty well that night. In the other ring, twelve clowns (33)_____ (try) to stuff themselves into a small car while the stunt coordinator (34)_____ (yell) directions at them. At the same time, above the center ring, two tightrope walkers (35)_____ (already climb) their ladders and (36)_____ (just step) out onto the tightrope.

II.

Then it (37)_____ (happen). One of the tightrope walkers, who (38)_____ (catch) a cold a few days before, suddenly (39)_____ (sneeze). He (40)_____ (lose) his balance and (41)_____ (crash) into the safety net. His partner (42)_____ (look) down for just a second, and then he (43)_____ (lose) his balance, too. He (44)_____ (catch) the tightrope with his right hand as he (45)_____ (fall), and he (46)_____ (hang) there for several seconds, trying to figure out what to do next. He (47)_____ (sweat) with fear because he (48)_____ (see) that the safety net (49)_____ (collapse) just after his partner (50)_____ (fall) into it. The audience, horrified, (51)_____ (hold) its breath.

The tightrope walker (52)_____ (cling) to the rope for as long as possible, and then he (53)_____ (let) go. I (54)_____ (be) sure that I (55)_____ (faint). The whole audience (56)_____ (know) that the poor guy (57)_____ (probably break) his neck in the fall.

However, instead of crashing to his death, he (58)_____ (fall) onto one of the elephants, (59)_____ (slide) off the elephant's back, and (60)_____ (land) softly on the floor of the tent. He (61)_____ (be) fine, but the elephant, shocked by this unexpected creature on her back, (62)_____ (flee) to the next ring, where the clowns (63)_____ (just squeeze) into the car and (64)_____ (now try) to wiggle out. The elephant (65)_____ (run) past the clowns toward the ringmaster, who (66)_____ (split) his pants while he (67)_____ (try) to climb over a low wall to get away.

Then the elephant (68)_____ (head) for the ring with the lions, where the lion tamer (69)_____ (run) back and forth, trying to capture his lions and put them back in their cages. I (70)_____ (wonder) what (71)_____ (happen) next when the lions, nervous and confused, (72)_____ (spring) out of the ring, into the audience. Terrified people (73)_____ (flee) in all directions. Others (74)_____ (hide) under their seats. Nobody (75)_____ (be) hurt, but several days later, the owners of the circus (76)_____ (choose) to go out of business because this kind of thing (77)_____ (forever happen).

III.

My short career with the circus (78)_____ (begin) and (79)_____ (end) over two decades ago. I (80)_____ (wait on) tables for a few years after finishing high school, and then I (81)_____ (go) to college. I (82)_____ (work) in a bank ever since I (83)_____ (graduate) from college. It (84)_____ (be) a very boring line of work. I (85)_____ (sit) at a desk all day and seldom (86)_____ (have) an opportunity to meet any interesting people. I (87)_____ (answer) questions and (88)_____ (give) financial advice whenever anyone (89)_____ (come) in and (90)_____ (ask) for a loan. Last year, one of the bank tellers (91)_____ (steal) $20,000 from the bank, and this year, three people (92)_____ (try) to rob the bank, but aside from that, nothing exciting ever (93)_____ (happen). Right now, for example, I (94)_____ (sit) at my desk and (95)_____ (hope) that the phone won't ring. I (96)_____ (think) about doing

something exciting: going on a safari through the jungle, taking a spaceship into outer space, or doing scientific experiments in a laboratory. You see, I (97)_____ (begin) to get very restless. I (98)_____ (wear) a business suit every business day for the past twenty years. I (99)_____ (answer) the same questions thousands of times. I (100)_____ (not do) anything exciting since I was a teenager. A good salary (101)_____ (not be) enough. I (102)_____ (see) circus posters all over town this week, and I (103)_____ (already decide) to put in my application and trade in my business suit for a clown suit!

Rap It Up

Telling about an Event. In a group of three students, describe the following events. Each student should take a different point of view of the same event. Tell the other students (1) where you were, (2) what you saw, (3) how you felt, (4) what you were doing at the time, (5) what you thought was going to happen, (6) what you did, (7) how this has changed your life, and (8) what you've been doing since then. Use your imagination!

1.   A Circus Performance

Student A	**Student B**	**Student C**
You were in the audience at the performance	You were the ringmaster of the circus.	You were a tightrope walker in the performance.

2.   A Bank Robbery

Student A	**Student B**	**Student C**
You were a customer standing in line at the bank.	You were a bank teller.	You were the bank robber.

3.   A Similar Situation of Your Own

Rap in the Real World

Interview. Choose a job that you hope to have someday. Work with a partner and tell this student something about the job. Then role-play a job interview.

Example: **A:** What kind of work are you doing now?
B: Well, I'm unemployed at the moment.
A: Have you worked as a _____ before?
B: Yes, I've has a lot of experience.

And so on.

FUTURE

13 = SIMPLE FUTURE: WILL/BE GOING TO =

Read the story on the left. When you finish, go back to the beginning, cover up the story on the left, and choose the correct tense for each capitalized simple form of the verb to the right of the picture.

—Good evening, ladies and gentlemen. Tonight, you*'re going to hear* what the candidates have to say.

The Save Our Planet Club welcomes the candidates. I'm sure that tonight *will be* informative for all of us.

We have several speakers. Ms. Kent *will* you *begin*, please?

—Thank you. Ladies and gentlemen, you*'re going to make* a very important choice next Tuesday. The choice *will be* yours.

—Good evening, ladies and gentlemen. Tonight, you HEAR what the candidates have to say.

The Save Our Planet Club welcomes the candidates. I'm sure that tonight BE informative for all of us.

We have several speakers. Ms. Kent, you BEGIN, please?

—Thank you. Ladies and gentlemen, you MAKE a very important choice next Tuesday. The choice BE yours.

If you elect me, I *will work* to protect the environment for future generations.

I *will make* sure that we preserve our beautiful forests for our great-grandchildren.

Mr. Talamany, on the other hand, *is going to turn* our forests into high-rise buildings, parking lots . . .

. . . and resort hotels for the very rich.

I *will do* everything possible to stop factories from polluting our air and water.

I *will stop* the oil companies from drilling in the ocean off of our beautiful shore.

If you elect me, I WORK to protect the environment for future generations.

I MAKE sure that we preserve our beautiful forests for our great-grandchildren.

Mr. Talamany, on the other hand, TURN our forests into high-rise buildings, parking lots . . .

. . . and resort hotels for the very rich.

I DO everything possible to stop factories from polluting our air and water.

I STOP the oil companies from drilling in the ocean off of our beautiful shore.

Mr. Talamany says he *will work* for the environment. But, as we've seen in the past, he hasn't shown much interest.

Are you *going to let* our environment be destroyed by greedy developers . . . or *are* you *going to vote* for me next Tuesday?

—Thank you, Ms. Kent. Mr. Talamany, *will* you *respond*, please?

Er . . . Mr. Talamany?

—Thank you. Ladies and gentlemen, I*'m going to tell* you why I'm the best candidate for the job.

I *will lower* unemployment in our city . . .

Mr. Talamany says he WORK for the environment. But, as we've seen in the past, he hasn't shown much interest.

You LET our environment be destroyed by greedy developers . . . or you VOTE for me next Tuesday?

—Thank you, Ms. Kent. Mr. Talamany, you RESPOND, please?

Er . . . Mr. Talamany?

—Thank you. Ladies and gentlemen, I TELL you why I'm the best candidate for the job.

I LOWER unemployment in our city . . .

... by beginning construction of a wonderful multi-million-dollar resort ...

... and a new oil refinery ...

... which *will process* the oil that we *will find* off of our own shore!

I*'m not going to stand by* and *watch* environmentalists ruin our economy!

What??!? You mean this isn't the Young Industrialists' Club?

THE END

... by beginning construction of a wonderful multi-million-dollar resort ...

... and a new oil refinery ...

... which PROCESS the oil that we FIND off of our own shore!

I NOT STAND BY and WATCH environmentalists ruin our economy!

What??!? You mean this isn't the Young Industrialists' Club?

FUTURE: WILL + SIMPLE FORM	FUTURE: BE GOING TO + SIMPLE FORM

NOW   FUTURE

	FUTURE: WILL + SIMPLE FORM	FUTURE: BE GOING TO + SIMPLE FORM
1.	**Will** (+ **simple form**) indicates *promise, determination, volunteered action, prediction,* or *inevitability* for the future. Your money *will disappear.* (prediction) ⟶ We*'ll need* more schools. (inevitability) ⟶ I*'ll spend* your money carefully. (promise) This city *will hire* as many people as ⟶ possible. (determination)	**Be going to** (+ **simple form**) indicates *prediction* and *inevitability* but not *promise, volunteered action,* or (usually) *determination.* = Your money *is going to disappear.* (prediction) = We*'re going to need* more schools. (inevitability) (See "By the Way. . . ," page 103.)
2.	We do not use **will** for an action or event planned for the future.	**Be going to** indicates an action or event *planned* with some certainty for the future. *Are* you *going to vote* for me? I*'m going to vote* for Ms. Kent.
3.	In the negative, **will not** (**won't**) can mean *refusal,* besides the negative of the meanings above in 1. I *won't let* this happen. = I refuse to let this happen.	**Be going to** can also indicate *refusal.* I*'m not going to let* this happen. = I refuse to let this happen.
4.	**Will** is used in polite requests and invitations. In this usage, it is interchangeable with *would* and *could.* *Will* you *begin,* please?	We do not use **be going to** for requests and invitations.
5.	**Shall** (another form of **will**) in American English is mainly used with *I* or *we* in the question form: *Shall* I *tell* you what we need? *Shall* we *begin*? (In statements, **shall** is considered very formal in American English.)	

Figure It Out

With a partner, study these sentences. What does *will* or *be going to* mean in each sentence? Write the meaning(s) on the chart. Then answer this question: Is it possible to use both forms of the future and keep the same meaning?

	Meaning(s)	Both *will* and *be going to* possible?
1. I*'ll give* it to them.		
2. The debate *is going to be* interesting.		
3. The population *will increase*.		
4. We *will protect* the environment.		
5. What *are* you *going to do* tonight?		
6. I*'ll give* her a call this evening.		
7. We*'re going to go* sailing next weekend.		
8. We *won't allow* that company to destroy the forest.		
9. He*'ll* really *like* this gift.		
10. I*'m going to clean* out my closet tomorrow.		

Rap It Up

A. Oral Practice. Laura Kent has worked hard in her campaign. Next week she's going to take a vacation. Using the pictures below, tell about her plans.

B. Practice. Pretend you are running for public office. Use the following phrases and some of your own to make campaign promises.

Phrases

build more schools
promote better education
clean up the city
provide jobs
help the needy

put in new street lights
send criminals to jail
lower taxes
balance the budget
listen to the voters

Fill It In

Tenses in Context. Fill in the blanks in the following story with the **future** tense using either "will" or "be going to." Remember that more than one tense is possible in some of the blanks.

Another Political Campaign

Lionel is running for president of his elementary school. He (1)_____ (be) in the sixth grade next year. He thinks he (2)_____ (be) very important then. Lionel promises to help all students. He says he (3)_____ (fire) all the cooks and (4)_____ (hire) new ones. His new cooks (5)_____ (fix) cheeseburgers, hot dogs, and French fries. They (6)_____ (serve) ice cream sundaes and chocolate cake for dessert every day. Lionel says that if he is elected, the school (7)_____ (have) longer recesses and shorter class sessions. He (8)_____ (cut) the school day in half. That way, he says, everyone (9)_____ (have) more time to play ball and to do other important things.

Lionel (10)_____ (work) hard to win this election. He (11)_____ (give) a speech at every recess. He (12)_____ (promise) new balls and a larger play yard. He says he (13)_____ (make) the school principal provide computer games and lots of new toys for everyone. The school (14)_____ (provide) snacks for every recess.

After school today, Lionel (15)_____ (stop) off at the stationery store. He (16)_____ (buy) cardboard, crayons, and glue. Then, at home, he (17)_____ (work) on his campaign posters. He (18)_____ (draw) pictures of the school on some posters and (19)_____ (glue) photographs of himself onto others. His posters (20)_____ (say) that he (21)_____ (cut out) homework and tests. Students (22)_____ (be able) to grade themselves. The teachers (23)_____ (have to) make every class interesting, or the students (24)_____ (find) a new teacher.

Lionel (25)_____ (be) very busy on election day. He (26)_____ (give) every student who votes for him a piece of bubble gum. That way, he (27)_____ (be) sure to win.

Rap in the Real World

Work with a partner. Talk about the coming week. Be sure to include plans, predictions, promises, things you're determined to do, and things that are inevitable. Use both "will" and "be going to." Listen to your partner carefully so that you can ask questions for further information.

Example: **A:** What are you going to do next Monday?
               B: I'm going to go to the doctor.

14

Read the story on the left. When you finish, go back to the beginning, cover up the story on the left, and choose the correct tense for each capitalized simple form of the verb to the right of the picture.

—So! Robert and Suzanne, you*'re going to get* married, and you want to know your future.

—So! Robert and Suzanne, you GET married, and you want to know your future.

I*'ll look* into my crystal ball and *tell* you everything.

I LOOK into my crystal ball and TELL you everything.

Your wedding *begins* at 2:00 next Saturday. But—oh dear—I see that Suzanne *will be* late.

Your wedding BEGIN at 2:00 next Saturday. But—oh dear—I see that Suzanne BE late.

Just before she *gets* to the church, Robert's nephew *is going to swallow* the wedding ring. You*'ll have to* use Robert's high school ring, instead.

Just before she GET to the church, Robert's nephew SWALLOW the wedding ring. You HAVE TO use Robert's high school ring, instead.

When the ceremony *is over*, you*'ll leave* for your honeymoon. Your plane *takes off* at 6:00.

Unfortunately, you *won't be able* to go to Hawaii because Robert *will lose* the tickets before your taxi *reaches* the airport.

Oh, dear. You*'ll spend* your honeymoon at a miserable, cold hotel downtown instead of going to Hawaii.

Suzanne *is going to catch* a terrible cold and *sneeze* for three straight days before you both *give up* and *go* home.

Tsk, tsk. As soon as you *move* into your little house, Robert, your brother *will lose* his job and *move* in with you.

He's *going to bring* his wife, four kids, dog, and cat with him.

When the ceremony BE over, you LEAVE for your honeymoon. Your plane TAKE OFF at 6:00.

Unfortunately, you NOT BE ABLE to go to Hawaii because Robert LOSE the tickets before your taxi REACH the airport.

Oh, dear. You SPEND your honeymoon at a miserable, cold hotel downtown instead of going to Hawaii.

Suzanne CATCH a terrible cold and SNEEZE for three straight days before you both GIVE UP and GO home.

Tsk, tsk. As soon as you MOVE into your little house, Robert, your brother LOSE his job and MOVE in with you.

He BRING his wife, four kids, dog, and cat with him.

Unfortunately, your house *won't be* a very quiet place until he *finds* a job and *moves* out.

But, on the other hand, things *will get* better. Soon after your children *are* born, you and Robert *are going to buy* a small grocery store and *fix* it up.

You*'ll work* very hard for several years.

Unless something very unusual *happens*, your little store *will become* a success.

As soon as you *save* enough money, you*'ll buy* another store, and another, and another, and another.

You*'ll own* a chain of supermarkets by the time your kids *finish* college.

Unfortunately, your house NOT BE a very quiet place until he FIND a job and MOVE out.

But, on the other hand, things GET better. Soon after your children BE born, you and Robert BUY a small grocery store and FIX it up.

You WORK very hard for several years.

Unless something very unusual HAPPEN, your little store BECOME a success.

As soon as you SAVE enough money, you BUY another store, and another, and another, and another.

You OWN a chain of supermarkets by the time your kids FINISH college.

Soon after you *open* your fourteenth store, you*'ll move* into a big mansion.

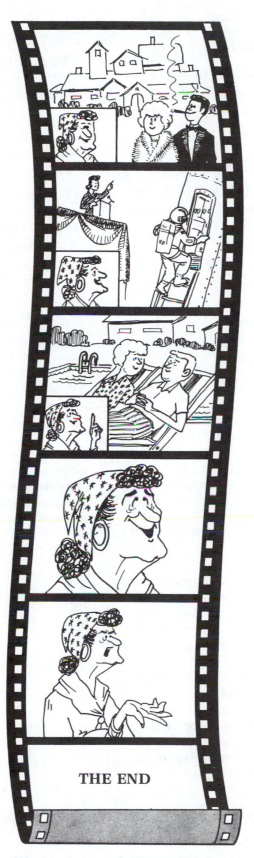

Soon after you OPEN your fourteenth store, you MOVE into a big mansion.

Your daughter *will become* president of the country, and your son *is going to explore* outer space.

Your daughter BECOME president of the country, and your son EXPLORE outer space.

When you*'re* old, you*'ll sit* by the pool and *remember* the past.

When you BE old, you SIT by the pool and REMEMBER the past.

You*'re going to be* rich. Your kids *are going to be* famous.

You BE rich. Your kids BE famous.

That'll be $10.00.

That'll be $10.00.

THE END

SIMPLE PRESENT	SIMPLE FUTURE: WILL / BE GOING TO

On a time line, the **simple present** (meaning the future) looks like the other future tenses. However, it is used differently.

```
        |                          ×
_____|_____×_____
      NOW                       FUTURE
```

1.

The **simple present** has a future meaning in subordinate clauses that express *time* and *condition* with these words:

when
whenever
while
as (= while)
until   } TIME
before
after
as soon as
by the time

if
unless   } CONDITION
in case

Unless something unusual *happens,* your store will become a success.

As soon as you *save* enough money, you'll buy another store.

The subordinate clause may come before the main clause (see the examples above), in which case there is a comma, or it may come after the main clause, in which case there is no comma:

Your store will become a success unless something unusual *happens.*

The **present perfect** is sometimes used instead of the **simple present** in a clause. It emphasizes completion of the activity in the clause.

As soon as you *'ve saved* enough money, you'll buy another store.

Will or **be going to** is used in the main clause of a future tense sentence that contains a subordinate clause of *time* or *condition.*

The main clause determines the tense of the whole sentence:

When the ceremony *is* over, the couple *leaves* for the honeymoon. = **present** (after *every* wedding)

When the ceremony *is* over, the couple *will leave* for the honeymoon. = **future** (after *this* wedding)

Although **will** or **be going to** or the **present continuous** (see Chapter 15) may be used in the main clause, **will** is perhaps most commonly used, even when it expresses a *plan.*

SIMPLE PRESENT	SIMPLE FUTURE: WILL / BE GOING TO
2. The **simple present** has a *future meaning* with certain specific verbs that indicate a *scheduled event*: start begin end open close arrive leave take off (meaning *leave*) get (to) (meaning *arrive*) land (meaning *arrive*) rise (the sun, a theater curtain) set (the sun) The wedding *begins* at 2:00 next Saturday. (scheduled event) The plane *takes off* at 6:00.	**Will** and **be going to** are not incorrect with these verbs, but they are less common and less natural. *I'm going to begin* that book soon. (not a scheduled event) *I'll take off* my coat. (not a scheduled event)

Picture Puzzle

Tenses in Context. As before, write out the following story, changing all of the pictures and symbols to words. The character's name is Esmeralda, but you should use pronouns whenever possible. For each of the circled verbs, choose the **simple future** tense (**will** or **be going to**) or the **simple present** tense (meaning the future). In many cases, both forms of the are possible.

Esmeralda is looking into her crystal ball to see her own future. What does she see?

Gypsy Esmeralda's Future

🔮 SEES THAT 🔮 (HAVE) PROBLEMS W/ 💵 ⊠ THE FUTURE IF SHE ~~CHANGE~~

HER WAY OF DOING BUSINESS. 🔮 (HAVE) 3 MAIN PROBLEMS.

1ST, 👪 (BEGIN) → DRIVE 🚐 HER LITTLE SHOP 🏠 THEIR WAY → BIG SHOPPING

CENTERS. 👪 (SEE) HER [FORTUNES $10°°] ⊠ THE 🏬 ⊠ THEIR HURRY → GET → A BIG

STORE.

ANOTHER PROBLEM (BE) HER 👁 SIGHT. AS 🔮 (GET) OLDER, HER 👁 SIGHT

(GET) WORSE. ⊠ THE FUTURE, IT (BE) DIFFICULT FOR HER → SEE IMAGES ⊠ HER

🔮 .

BUT [gypsy]'S WORST PROBLEM (BE) THAT [people] (STOP) BELIEVING [x] GYPSIES w/ [crystal ball]S BECAUSE [people] (THINK) THAT [crystal ball]S ARE OUT OF STYLE. WHEN [people] (DO) THAT, [people] (STOP) GOING → FORTUNE-TELLERS, & [gypsy]'S BUSINESS (BE) [x] TERRIBLE TROUBLE. YOUNG [people] (B̶E̶G̶) HER FOR ADVICE [box] ROMANCE ANYMORE. ROCK STARS (O̶F̶F̶E̶R̶) HER [money] & JEWELRY FOR ADVICE [box] [music]. DETECTIVES (A̶S̶K̶) HER FOR HELP [x] CATCHING CRIMINALS.

AS SOON AS [gypsy] (MAKE) SOME BIG CHANGES [x] HER BUSINESS, [gypsy] (STOP) WORRYING, & [gypsy] (H̶A̶V̶E̶) ANY MORE TROUBLE w/ ULCERS. BUT BECAUSE [gypsy] (ALWAYS BE) A STUBBORN, INDEPENDENT [woman], [gypsy] (REFUSE) → MAKE ANY CHANGES UNTIL THE [city] GOVERNMENT (DECIDE) → EVICT HER & TEAR ↓ HER [house]. WHEN THEY (DO) THAT, [gypsy] (HAVE TO) MOVE HER BUSINESS → A SHOPPING CENTER. AFTER [gypsy] (MOVE), [gypsy] (GET) SOME [loan] & (BUY) ADVERTISING [x] ALL THE LOCAL [newspaper]S. THEN [gypsy] (THROW) [out] HER [crystal ball] & (BUY) A [computer].

AS SOON AS A CUSTOMER (SEE) HER [computer], [person] (KNOW) THAT [gypsy] IS A VERY MODERN FORTUNE-TELLER. SOON, 1,000 s OF [people] (BEGIN) → COME → HER NEW SHOP. [gypsy] (HIRE) MORE [people] & (OPEN) BRANCH OFFICES. EVERY OFFICE (HAVE) A [computer]. [x] A FEW YEARS, [gypsy] (HAVE) A WHOLE [chain] OF OFFICES, & BUSINESS (BE) TERRIFIC!

Rap It Up

Oral Practice. Pretend you are a fortune-teller. Tell the fortunes of the following people by combining the words from the list on the next page with as many pictures to the right of the list as possible. Finish the sentence with a prediction.

Examples: If she goes on a cruise, she'll meet the man of her dreams.
He'll meet the girl of his dreams when he goes on a cruise.
Before they go on a cruise, they'll . . .

If
After
As soon as
Before
Unless
By the time
While
When
In case

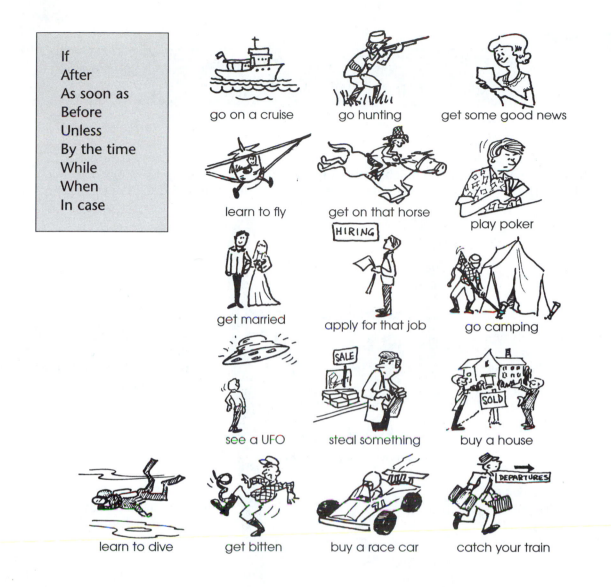

go on a cruise

go hunting

get some good news

learn to fly

get on that horse

play poker

get married

apply for that job

go camping

see a UFO

steal something

buy a house

learn to dive

get bitten

buy a race car

catch your train

Rap in the Real World

A. Work in small groups. Make predictions about each others' lives.

Example: **A:** I think that when you . . .
          B: And after that, what am I going to do?

B. Work with a partner. Make predictions about your own life.

15

PRESENT CONTINUOUS (meaning the future)

SIMPLE FUTURE: WILL/BE GOING TO

Read the story on the left. When you finish, go back to the beginning, cover up the story on the left, and choose the correct tense for each capitalized simple form of the verb to the right of the picture.

THE STUNT MAN

—Ah! Good! You're our new stunt person! You*'ll be* pretty busy today. We*'re going to begin* in about an hour.

—Ah! Good! You're our new stunt person! You BE pretty busy today. We BEGIN in about an hour.

—Great! I*'m* really *going to enjoy* working with you experienced stunt people. What *are* we *doing* today?

—Great! I really ENJOY working with you experienced stunt people. What we DO today?

—Well, you*'ll be* on top of that building and I*'ll be* down here.

—Well, you BE on top of that building and I BE down here.

You*'re going to fight* with that guy over there, and he*'ll punch* you in the face.

You FIGHT with that guy over there, and he PUNCH you in the face.

114 TENSE SITUATIONS

You*'re going to fall* off the
building. Remember that
you*'ll need* to look scared
while you*'re falling.*

You FALL off the building.
Remember that you NEED
to look scared while you
FALL.

—Oh, I*'ll remember.*

—Oh, I REMEMBER.

—After that, we*'re having* a
car crash. You*'re going to
drive* this car off that cliff
into the lake.

—After that, we HAVE a car
crash. You DRIVE this car
off that cliff into the lake.

—Which car *are* **you**
driving?

—Which car **you** DRIVE?

—I*'m* not *driving* a car. I'm
the stunt coordinator.
Whenever you*'re doing* a
stunt, I*'ll have* to watch and
take notes. Now, let me
explain this.

—I not DRIVE a car. I'm the
stunt coordinator. Whenever
you DO a stunt, I HAVE to
watch and take notes. Now,
let me explain this.

Be sure not to lose control
of the car until you*'re going*
80 miles per hour.

Be sure not to lose control
of the car until you GO 80
miles per hour.

You'*ll hit* that rock, and the car *will roll* over.

You HIT that rock, and the car ROLL over.

The car *will land* in the lake and *start* to sink. While it'*s sinking,* you'*re going to crawl* out and *cling* to the top of the car.

The car LAND in the lake and START to sink. While it SINK, you CRAWL out and CLING to the top of the car.

Make sure that you look miserable while you'*re clinging* to the car.

Make sure that you look miserable while you CLING to the car.

—Oh, that *won't be* hard. I'*ll look* miserable.

—Oh, that NOT BE hard. I LOOK miserable.

—Good. Hmmm. Let me see. What *are* we *doing* next?

—Good. Hmmm. Let me see. What we DO next?

—**We?**

—**We?**

—**You**. Ah, yes. You*'re going to jog* down the street.

As you*'re jogging*, a lion *will growl* at you from behind that tree.

It's important for you to look nervous while he*'s attacking* you.

—Attacking me? Listen. I have my own plan for these stunts. I*'m not falling* off any building. I*'m not driving* a car off any cliff. And no lion *is attacking* me!

—Ah! Good! You're our new stunt person! You*'ll be* pretty busy today. We*'re going to begin* in about an hour.

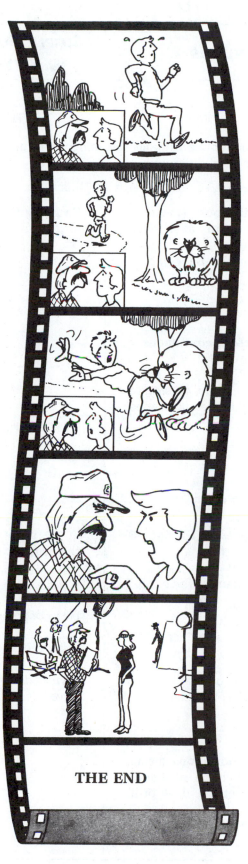

THE END

—**You**. Ah, yes. You JOG down the street.

As you JOG, a lion GROWL at you from behind that tree.

It's important for you to look nervous while he ATTACK you.

—Attacking me? Listen. I have my own plan for these stunts. I NOT FALL off any building. I NOT DRIVE a car off any cliff. And no lion ATTACK me!

—Ah! Good! You're our new stunt person! You BE pretty busy today. We BEGIN in about an hour.

PRESENT CONTINUOUS	SIMPLE FUTURE: WILL / BE GOING TO

NOW ———————×———— FUTURE

On a time line, the **present continuous** (meaning the future) looks like the other future tenses. However, it is used differently.

1.

The **present continuous** (meaning the future) is used for a *planned* future action or event. It is generally interchangeable with the **be going to** form.

What *are* we *doing* next?

Exceptions: The **present continuous** is not used for the future with:

a. verbs such as *rain*, *snow*, *get sick*, or *die* because these aren't planned events, and

b. NON-ACTION verbs. (See pages 9–11.)

Be going to (but not **will**) is also used for a future *plan*.

What *are* we *going to do* next?

2.

In the negative, the **present continuous** indicates:

a. the negative of a plan for the future:

He's *not coming* tomorrow.

b. refusal:

I'm *not driving* this car off that cliff. = I refuse to drive this car off that cliff.

In the negative, **be going to** indicates the negative of a plan for the future:

He's *not going to come* tomorrow.

Both **will** and **be going to** are used for refusal:
I *won't drive* this car. = I'm *not going to drive* this car. = I refuse to drive this car.

3.

When the **present continuous** means the future, some indication of time is given in either the sentence itself or in the whole context:

PRESENT CONTINUOUS	SIMPLE FUTURE: WILL / BE GOING TO
—What *are* you *doing* tomorrow? (sentence) —I'*m starting* a new job as a stunt man. (context)	
4. The **present continuous** is often used in subordinate clauses that express *time* and *condition* with these words: when while as (= while) until by the time if unless in case Whenever you'*re doing* a stunt, I'*ll watch* and *take* notes. You'll need to look scared while you'*re falling.* **Note:** Sometimes the **present continuous** is used in the main clause. When it is, some indication of time is usually in the sentence. We'*re discussing* it tomorrow while we're driving to work.	We usually use **will** or **be going to** in the main clauses of sentences with subordinate clauses of *time* or *condition.* Whenever you're doing a stunt, I'*ll watch* and *take* notes.

Rap It Up

Oral Practice. The chart on the following page is the stunt man's schedule for next week. Ask your partner questions about the schedule using **will/be going to** or the **present continuous** tense.

<u>**Examples:**</u> What is he going to do at ten o'clock on Monday?
Where is he going at one o'clock on Monday?

	Monday	Tuesday	Wednesday	Thursday	Friday
9:00	drive a car into the ocean	spread a net across the street		chase a thief	float down rapids on a raft
10:00	thrash about in water as if drowning		take flying lessons		dive off a cliff
11:00		climb a skyscraper		run away from bears	
12:00	fight off sharks		fly a plane over the Himalayas		ride a motorcycle
1:00	go to a seafood restaurant	fight criminals on a skyscraper		shoot a lion	
2:00			crash a plane into a mountain		drown in lake
3:00	swim laps to get in shape		jump out of a burning plane		
4:00	review a film	jump off a building		do retakes of a movie	swing across the jungle on a rope

Rap in the Real World

Ask your partner questions about his or her week's schedule.

Example: What are you doing tomorrow at three o'clock?

Fill It In

Tenses in Context. Fill in the blanks in the following story with the **future tense** (**will** or **be going to**) or the **present continuous**. Remember that more than one tense may be possible in some of the blanks.

Johnny, the new stunt man, decided that he didn't like that business very much. He has now decided to learn to become a roofer.

The Roofing Business

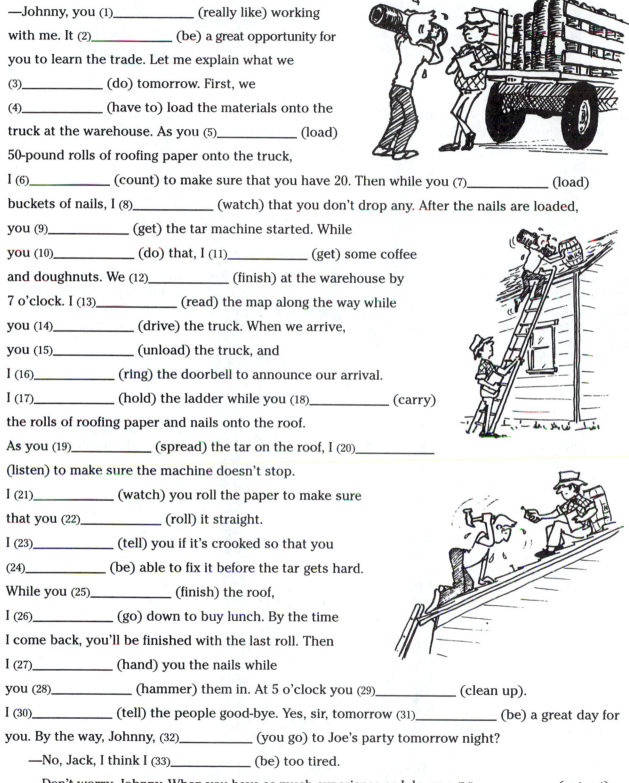

—Johnny, you (1)_____ (really like) working with me. It (2)_____ (be) a great opportunity for you to learn the trade. Let me explain what we (3)_____ (do) tomorrow. First, we (4)_____ (have to) load the materials onto the truck at the warehouse. As you (5)_____ (load) 50-pound rolls of roofing paper onto the truck, I (6)_____ (count) to make sure that you have 20. Then while you (7)_____ (load) buckets of nails, I (8)_____ (watch) that you don't drop any. After the nails are loaded, you (9)_____ (get) the tar machine started. While you (10)_____ (do) that, I (11)_____ (get) some coffee and doughnuts. We (12)_____ (finish) at the warehouse by 7 o'clock. I (13)_____ (read) the map along the way while you (14)_____ (drive) the truck. When we arrive, you (15)_____ (unload) the truck, and I (16)_____ (ring) the doorbell to announce our arrival. I (17)_____ (hold) the ladder while you (18)_____ (carry) the rolls of roofing paper and nails onto the roof. As you (19)_____ (spread) the tar on the roof, I (20)_____ (listen) to make sure the machine doesn't stop. I (21)_____ (watch) you roll the paper to make sure that you (22)_____ (roll) it straight. I (23)_____ (tell) you if it's crooked so that you (24)_____ (be) able to fix it before the tar gets hard. While you (25)_____ (finish) the roof, I (26)_____ (go) down to buy lunch. By the time I come back, you'll be finished with the last roll. Then I (27)_____ (hand) you the nails while you (28)_____ (hammer) them in. At 5 o'clock you (29)_____ (clean up). I (30)_____ (tell) the people good-bye. Yes, sir, tomorrow (31)_____ (be) a great day for you. By the way, Johnny, (32)_____ (you go) to Joe's party tomorrow night?

— No, Jack, I think I (33)_____ (be) too tired.

— Don't worry, Johnny. When you have as much experience as I do, you (34)_____ (not get) tired out so easily.

Read the following story. When you finish, go back to the beginning, cover up the story on the left, and choose the correct tense for each capitalized simple form of the verb to the right of the picture.

A NEW BROTHER

—Well, Lupita, tomorrow we *'re going to bring* your mother and new little brother, Carlito, home from the hospital.

—Well, Lupita, tomorrow we BRING your mother and new little brother, Carlito, home from the hospital.

It *'s going to be* wonderful having a new family member.

It BE wonderful having a new family member.

You *'ll be helping* your mother take care of Carlito while he *'s growing up*.

You HELP your mother take care of Carlito while he GROW UP.

He *'ll grow* very quickly. When he is four months old, he *'ll be rolling* over.

He GROW very quickly. When he is four months old, he ROLL over.

He*'ll be getting* his first cute little tooth at around six months.

At seven months he*'ll be crawling*.

Then he*'ll learn* to walk. While he*'s taking* his first step, we*'ll* all *be watching*.

While he*'s learning* to walk, he*'ll be falling down* a lot.

He*'ll fall down*, and you*'ll pick* him *up*.

As he*'s getting* older, you*'ll be lending* him your toys.

He GET his first cute little tooth at around six months.

At seven months he CRAWL.

Then he LEARN to walk. While he TAKE his first step, we all WATCH.

While he LEARN to walk, he FALL DOWN a lot.

He FALL DOWN, and you PICK him UP.

As he GET older, you LEND him your toys.

He*'ll wind up* your toys for you.

You*'ll be blowing up* balloons for him to play with.

It*'ll be* fun having a brother to do things with.

We*'ll be taking* him to the beach often next summer. You*'ll be teaching* him how to swim while we're there.

He*'s going to be watching* you while you*'re building* sand castles.

You*'ll build* sand castles, and then he*'ll play* with them.

He WIND UP your toys for you.

You BLOW UP balloons for him to play with.

It BE fun having a brother to do things with.

We TAKE him to the beach often next summer. You TEACH him how to swim while we're there.

He WATCH you while you BUILD sand castles.

You BUILD sand castles, and then he PLAY with them.

We*'ll* also *be taking* him to the park. He*'ll go* down the slide and you*'ll catch* him.

We also TAKE him to the park. He GO down the slide and you CATCH him.

Then when he*'s learning* to ride a bicycle, you*'ll be running* alongside him.

Then when he LEARN to ride a bicycle, you RUN alongside him.

Before too long, you*'re going to be walking* him to school every day.

Before too long, you WALK him to school every day.

He*'ll be drawing* lots of pictures all through elementary school, and you*'ll be helping* him.

He DRAW lots of pictures all through elementary school, and you HELP him.

You*'re* really *going to appreciate* having a younger brother, Lupita . . . Lupita, where are you going?

You really APPRECIATE having a younger brother, Lupita . . . Lupita, where are you going?

THE END

FUTURE CONTINUOUS	SIMPLE FUTURE: WILL / BE GOING TO
1. There are two forms of the **future continuous**: will be (eating) be going to be (eating) These are generally interchangeable; however, the latter is rarely used because of its length.	See Chapter 13 for details.
2. The **future continuous** indicates an action that will be in progress at a definite time in the future. Next month, he'll *be crawling*. At midnight tomorrow, I'll *be hiding* under his crib.	When the action won't be repeated and will be at an indefinite or unknown future time, the **simple future** may also be used. Soon he'll *get* his first tooth. = Soon he'll *be getting* his first tooth.
3. The **future continuous** is also used for an action that will be in progress when another action happens. While he's taking his first step, we'll *be watching*.	The **simple future** is used for a future action that will happen after another future action. He'll *fall* down, and you'll *pick* him *up*.
4. The **future continuous** also emphasizes the (long) duration of a future action. He'll *be drawing* all day long.	

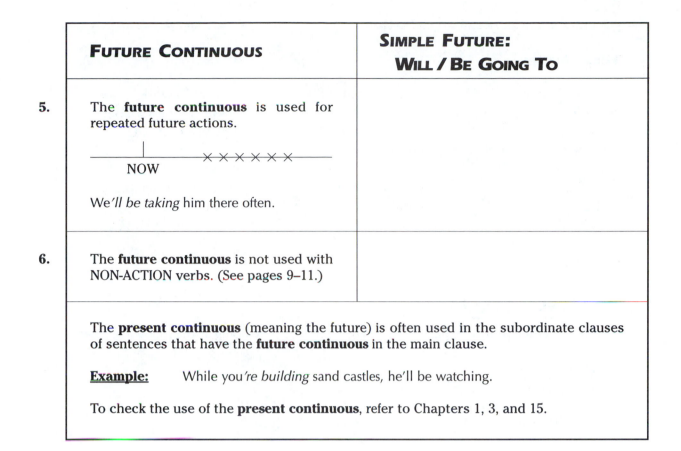

	FUTURE CONTINUOUS	SIMPLE FUTURE: WILL / BE GOING TO
5.	The **future continuous** is used for repeated future actions. ———|—×××××——— NOW We'*ll be taking* him there often.	
6.	The **future continuous** is not used with NON-ACTION verbs. (See pages 9–11.)	

The **present continuous** (meaning the future) is often used in the subordinate clauses of sentences that have the **future continuous** in the main clause.

Example: While you*'re building* sand castles, he'll be watching.

To check the use of the **present continuous**, refer to Chapters 1, 3, and 15.

Rap It Up

A. Oral Practice. Use the following time expressions and the verb phrases from Part B to make up sentences about Carlito's family. Use the **future continuous** tense.

Example: At 9:00 tomorrow morning, Carlito's father will be changing Carlito's diaper.

> ### Time Expressions
>
> 9:00 tomorrow morning   1:00 Monday morning
> dinner time   the day after tomorrow at 6:00
> 12:30 Saturday afternoon   breakfast time
> next Thursday evening at 7:00   11:00 tomorrow night
> 8:00 tomorrow evening   after lunch

B. Practice. Combine two phrases from the list on the following page to make sentences telling what Carlito's family will be doing. Use the **present continuous** and the **future continuous**. Also, use words such as *while, as,* and *when.*

Example: As Carlito's mother is rocking him, she will be singing.

Rap in the Real World

Work with a partner. Tell your partner what you think you'll be doing at the following times:

- next weekend
- next summer
- next year
- ten years from now
- in the year 2020

Picture Puzzle

Tenses in Context. On another piece of paper, write out the following story. Change the pictures and symbols to words. For each of the circled verbs, choose the **present continuous** (meaning the future), the **simple future** (**will** or **be going to**), or the **future continuous**. In some cases, more than one tense may be possible. The main character is the child from the earlier story.

🐟 = I (OR ME)   😊 = HE (OR HIM)

My Plan for My New Brother

MY PARENTS (BRING) MY NEW BABY BROTHER 🏠 FROM THE 🏢 TOMORROW

A.M. & LIFE (BE) JUST TERRIBLE FOR 🐟. MY PARENTS (P̶A̶Y̶) ANY ATTENTION → 🐟

ANYMORE. WHILE MY MOTHER (FEED) 😊 , 🐟 (DO) MY HOMEWORK W/OUT ANY HELP.

WHILE 🐟 (READ) MY SCHOOL 📖S OUT LOUD, MY FATHER (L̶I̶S̶T̶E̶N̶) BECAUSE HE

(PLAY) W/ MY BABY BROTHER. WHILE 🐟 (SWING) X THE BACKYARD, MY BROTHER

(CRAWL) ACROSS THE LAWN, SO MY PARENTS (WATCH) ME. AS MY BROTHER (GROW)

↑, 🐟 (SHRINK) X→ THE BACKGROUND.

HOWEVER, 🐟 HAVE A PLAN. @ 🕐 TOMORROW 🌙★, 😊 (HIDE) 💻 MY BROTHER'S

[bed], & [I] (WAIT) UNTIL MY PARENTS (SLEEP). THEN [I] (GRAB) MY BROTHER &

QUIETLY (CREEP) [out] OF THE [house]. [I] (GET) [in] A [bus] & TAKE [him] BACK → THE

[hospital]. [I] (TRADE) [him] [for] [in] SOMETHING ELSE: MAYBE A [dog] OR A [horse] OR A [robot].

[in] THE OTHER [hand], MAYBE [I] (STEAL) [him]. IF [I] DO, THE POLICE (PROBABLY ARREST)

[me] FOR KIDNAPPING. MY MOTHER (PROBABLY FAINT), & MY FATHER (YELL) A LOT &

(TEAR) [out] HIS HAIR. NO, [I] (TRADE) [him] [X]. INSTEAD, [I] (TEACH) [him] THINGS. FOR

EXAMPLE, [I] (TEACH) [him] → PLAY HIDE & SEEK. WHILE [I] (HIDE), [him] (LOOK) FOR [me].

AND [I] (TEACH) [him] → RIDE A [bike] & BUILD A TOY [house] & FLOAT [X] THE [boat]. [I] (TEACH)

[him] ABOUT THE [animals] [X] THE ZOO, TOO. OF COURSE, WHILE [him] (LEARN) ALL THESE

THINGS, MY PARENTS (IGNORE) [me]. [I] (TEACH) [him] ALL [day] LONG, BUT MY PARENTS

(PROBABLY THINK) HE'S A GENIUS.

[I] KNOW WHAT [I] (DO). [I] (RUN) AWAY FROM [home]! ONE [night], WHEN MY

PARENTS (SLEEP), [I] (PACK) MY [suitcase] & QUIETLY (CREEP) [out] OF THE [house]. [I] (GET)

A [bus] & (LEAVE) THE [city] FAR BEHIND. WHILE MY LITTLE BROTHER (GROW) ↑, [he]

(WISH) HE HAD A BIG SISTER → TEACH [him] ABOUT [bike]s & [boat]s & [animals]s

& PARENTS!

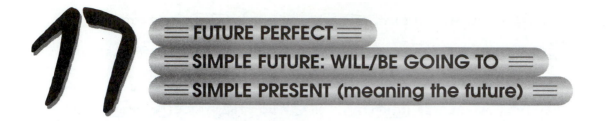

FUTURE PERFECT
SIMPLE FUTURE: WILL/BE GOING TO
SIMPLE PRESENT (meaning the future)

Read the story on the left. When you finish, go back to the beginning, cover up the story on the left, and choose the correct tense for each capitalized simple form of the verb to the right of the picture.

THE PLANS
OF A
JUNIOR
GENIUS

—I've always believed that it's important to plan for the future. I've been putting together some ideas for my "Life Schedule."

—I've always believed that it's important to plan for the future. I've been putting together some ideas for my "Life Schedule."

When I *graduate* from elementary school next month, I'*m going to celebrate* because I *will have finished* my first six years of school.

When I GRADUATE from elementary school next month, I CELEBRATE because I FINISH my first six years of school.

By graduation day, I *will have learned* to play chess.

By graduation day, I LEARN to play chess.

I also *will have done* a lot of experiments with my chemistry set and then *gotten* bored with it.

I also DO a lot of experiments with my chemistry set and then GET bored with it.

By the time I *finish* high school, I *will have taken* algebra, geometry, and calculus.

I'*ll* probably *give* the graduation speech because I *will have gotten* straight A's all through high school.

By graduation day, I *will have completed* my independent studies of animal behavior.

When I *graduate* from college, I'*ll get* a job as a math teacher.

By that time, I *will have become* the university chess champion and a computer expert.

When I *turn* 30, I'*m going to start* making plans for a new career because I probably *will have gotten* bored with my life.

By the time I FINISH high school, I TAKE algebra, geometry, and calculus.

I probably GIVE the graduation speech because I GET straight A's all through high school.

By graduation day, I COMPLETE my independent studies of animal behavior.

When I GRADUATE from college, I GET a job as a math teacher.

By that time, I BECOME the university chess champion and a computer expert.

When I TURN 30, I START making plans for a new career because I probably GET bored with my life.

I *will have taught* math at several universities . . .

. . . and *written* a lot of texts.

I hope that by that time I *will have won* an international chess tournament.

It*'ll be* time to move on to something completely new.

I think I*'m going to go* to Africa and *study* the animals there.

By the time I *come* home from my first safari, I *will have captured* thousands of creatures on film . . .

I TEACH math at several universities . . .

. . . and WRITE a lot of texts.

I hope that by that time I WIN an international chess tournament.

It BE time to move on to something completely new.

I think I GO to Africa and STUDY the animals there.

By the time I COME home from my first safari, I CAPTURE thousands of creatures on film . . .

... and I *will have gathered* a lot of information on wild animal behavior.

When my book of African photographs *is* published, I*'ll become* world famous.

Maybe I*'ll* even *win* awards for my genius with a camera.

—Billy, it's time to put away your toys and go to bed.

—When *is* the world *going to learn* to appreciate genius?

THE END

... and I GATHER a lot of information on wild animal behavior.

When my book of African photographs BE published, I BECOME world famous.

Maybe I EVEN WIN awards for my genius with a camera.

—Billy, it's time to put away your toys and go to bed.

—When the world LEARN to appreciate genius?

FUTURE PERFECT	SIMPLE FUTURE: WILL / BE GOING TO
1. The **future perfect** expresses an action that will end *before* another action in the future. That is, we use the **future perfect** when we "jump back" from another future time. NOW FUTURE PERFECT FUTURE When I turn 30, I *will have gotten* bored with my life. (**Note:** *when = before*)	We usually use the **simple future** if we move "forward" in time and if it is clear which action happened first. NOW FUTURE When I turn 30, I'*m going to start* making plans for a new career. (**Note:** *when = when* or *after*)
2. The **future perfect** doesn't always begin in the future. PAST NOW FUTURE When he retires next year, he *will have worked* here for 35 years. In this case, because the duration of time is emphasized, we often use the **future perfect continuous** instead. (See Chapter 18.)	For details on the **simple future**, see Chapter 13.

The **simple present** (meaning the future) is often used in the subordinate clauses of sentences that have the **future perfect** in the main clause.

<u>Example:</u>   When I graduate from college, I will have read every available book on higher mathematics.

The **present perfect** (meaning the future) is also sometimes used in the subordinate clause.

To check the use of the **simple present**, refer to Chapters 1, 2, and 14.

Fill It In

Tenses in Context. Fill in the blanks in the following story with the **future perfect**, **simple future**, or **simple present**. Remember that more than one tense may be possible in some of the blanks.

Mr. Adam's Class

It's another first day of school—the twentieth first day for Mr. Adams, the third-grade teacher. The school year no longer holds any surprises for him. He knows that by the end of the first day, at least two kids (1)_____ (run) home crying. Someone (2)_____ (stick) gum in the drinking fountain, and someone else (3)_____ (fall) asleep during his "first-day-of-school" lecture. By the time the final bell (4)_____ (ring), one or two kids (5)_____ (lose) their new notebooks. Several more (6)_____ (tear) their new school clothes.

The first week (7)_____ (finally come) to an end, and then it (8)_____ (be) time for serious business. By the end of the first month, Mr. Adams (9)_____ (hear) at least thirty different excuses for incomplete homework. At least half a dozen kids (10)_____ (not understand) three-fourths of the lessons. He (11)_____ (explain) the same points at least ten times each.

When Halloween (12)_____ (arrive), over half the class (13)_____ (get) sick from eating too much candy. It (14)_____ (take) at least a week before they (15)_____ (recover).

By Christmas, one-fourth of the students (16)_____ (fail) half the tests. After they (17)_____ (fail), all of them (18)_____ (promise) to do a better job during the new year.

When spring vacation (19)_____ (roll around), everyone (20)_____ (be) ready for a break. The students (21)_____ (complain) over and over about Mr. Adams being too strict. They (22)_____ (get) tired of doing homework. Mr. Adams (23)_____ (be) ready for his annual week at the health spa where he (24)_____ (sit) in the sauna and (25)_____ (sweat) out all his problems.

When they (26)_____ (return) to school after spring break, the students (27)_____ (forget) everything they learned before vacation. It (28)_____ (take) two weeks to return to normal.

By June, Mr. Adams (29)_____ (consider) retiring several times. He (30)_____ (swear) to quit at least two dozen times. But we all know that when school (31)_____ (begin) again next September, he (32)_____ (be) there ready for his new group of little "geniuses."

Rap It Up

Oral Practice. Below are some of the students in Billy's class. In the middle column are things they are going to do next year. In the column on the right are things they will have done by the time of their ten-year class reunion. Make sentences using the **simple future** and the **future perfect**.

<u>Examples:</u>   Jason is going to begin lifting weights next year.
               By the ten-year reunion, he will have won 3 Olympic gold medals for weightlifting.

	Next year	By 10-year reunion
Jason	begin lifting weights	win 3 Olympic gold medals for weightlifting
Richard	get braces	become a famous model
Maria	take singing lessons	become an opera singer
Sung-Sook	study chemistry	discover a cure for a rare disease
Armen	get a kitten for his birthday	become a lion tamer
Debbie	begin exercising	open her own health spa
Raffi	take swimming lessons	swim the English Channel
Heidi	begin sailing lessons	sail around the world
Hamid	climb trees with a friend	climb Mt. Everest
Amanda	practice writing	become a famous novelist

Rap in the Real World

A. Fill in your "life schedule" below. Use just the simple form of verbs in your notes. Use your imagination. In a group of three students, exchange your life schedules. Student A will ask Student B about Student C, Student B will ask Student C about Student A, and so on.

<u>Example:</u>   **A:** In five years, how many places will he have traveled to?
            B: He will have traveled to three different places.

	Next month	Next year	In 5 years	In 10 years
career	_____	_____	_____	_____
hobby	_____	_____	_____	_____
love life	_____	_____	_____	_____
travel	_____	_____	_____	_____
personal appearance	_____	_____	_____	_____

B. Predict world events that will begin in the year 2500 or that will have happened by then. Use the **simple future** and the **future perfect**.

Read the story on the left. When you finish, go back to the beginning, cover up the story on the left, and choose the correct tense for each capitalized simple form of the verb to the right of the picture.

LIFE
IN A
DIVING
BELL

Dear Mom,
    Guess what? We've finally figured out a way to get letters to the top. By the time you *receive* this letter, we *will have been living* in this diving bell for three years.

I know you*'ll be shaking* your head as you *read* this and *wondering* how I could consent to live under the ocean.

But, really, it's not as hard as you may think. By fall of next year we *will have been conducting* scientific research here for almost four years.

Besides, it's good to know that when we *leave* here we *won't have been wasting* the last few years; instead, we *will have been helping* to make humankind's knowledge of the marine world more complete.

Dear Mom,
    Guess what? We've finally figured out a way to get letters to the top. By the time you RECEIVE this letter, we LIVE in this diving bell for three years.

I know you SHAKE your head as you READ this and WONDER how I could consent to live under the ocean.

But, really, it's not as hard as you may think. By fall of next year we CONDUCT scientific research here for almost four years.

Besides, it's good to know that when we LEAVE here we NOT WASTE the last few years; instead, we HELP to make humankind's knowledge of the marine world more complete.

Our life in this little cell has now become almost routine. For example, tomorrow Leonard *will be working* outside on the ocean floor as usual.

He*'s going to be planting* the crops.

Of course, farming is not the only thing he*'ll be doing* tomorrow. He*'ll be exploring* parts of the ocean that are new to him and *searching* for new species of fish and plant life.

Here in the ocean he's not only a scientist and farmer; he's also a hunter. He hunts fish for food every day.

I worry about him because I know that by the time he *gets* home tomorrow evening, he *will have been fighting off* sharks all day in order to provide food for us.

It's good to know that when we *come* up for Thanksgiving next month, we*'ll be eating* turkey instead of fish.

Our life in this little cell has now become almost routine. For example, tomorrow Leonard WORK outside on the ocean floor as usual.

He PLANT the crops.

Of course, farming is not the only thing he DO tomorrow. He EXPLORE parts of the ocean that are new to him and SEARCH for new species of fish and plant life.

Here in the ocean he's not only a scientist and farmer; he's also a hunter. He hunts fish for food every day.

I worry about him because I know that by the time he GET home tomorrow evening, he FIGHT OFF sharks all day in order to provide food for us.

It's good to know that when we COME up for Thanksgiving next month, we EAT turkey instead of fish.

By that time I *will have been dreaming* about meat, French fries, and hot fudge sundaes for three years.

To help pass the time between now and then, I*'ll be fixing* seaweed cakes to bring up with us.

I*'m* also *going to be training* some dolphins to help protect us and our home.

They*'ll be guarding* our cell from any intruders.

You*'ll be wondering* by now about this cell we call home.

It is a fairly small one, with room only for a bed, a table, and a small area for exercising.

By that time I DREAM about meat, French fries, and hot fudge sundaes for three years.

To help pass the time between now and then, I FIX seaweed cakes to bring up with us.

I also TRAIN some dolphins to help protect us and our home.

They GUARD our cell from any intruders.

You WONDER by now about this cell we call home.

It is a fairly small one, with room only for a bed, a table, and a small area for exercising.

Soon, we're going to be building a new, more roomy place to live in.

When we come up, we'll be looking for building materials.

We'll also be shopping for clothes for the three of us.

Yes, mother, we have a little surprise for you.

On Thanksgiving you'll be meeting Erica, your new granddaughter.

Love,
Rebecca

Soon, we BUILD a new, more roomy place to live in.

When we COME up, we LOOK for building materials.

We also SHOP for clothes for the three of us.

Yes, mother, we have a little surprise for you.

On Thanksgiving you MEET Erica, your new granddaughter.

Love,
Rebecca

THE END

FUTURE PERFECT CONTINUOUS	FUTURE CONTINUOUS

1. The **future perfect continuous** emphasizes the (long) duration of an action or a habitual action *before* another time in the future. The length of time is usually given in the sentence. We often use *for* or *since* with the **future perfect continuous**.

NOW   FUTURE

By the time you receive this, we *will have been living* here for three years.

1. The **future continuous** emphasizes the duration of an action or a habitual action *at* or *after* another future time.

NOW   FUTURE

You*'ll be shaking* your head as you read this.

NOW   FUTURE

When we come, we*'ll be shopping* for building materials.

2. The **future perfect continuous** may begin at any time *before* the other future action; it may even begin in the past. Again, the length of time is usually given, often with *for* or *since*.

NOW   FUTURE

I *will have been dreaming* about hot fudge sundaes for three years.

2. The **future continuous** may be used alone, without another future time in the sentence. In this way, we may use the word *for* to indicate the length of time.

NOW

We*'ll be staying* with you for several weeks.

However, we do not use *since* with the **future continuous**.

For more on the **future continuous**, see Chapter 16.

3. We don't use either the **future perfect continuous** or the **future continuous** with NON-ACTION verbs. (See pages 9–11.)

4. The **simple present** (meaning the future) is often used in the subordinate clauses of sentences that have the **future perfect continuous** in the main clause.

By the time you receive this, we will have been living here for three years.
    (subordinate clause)   (main clause)

To check the usage of the **simple present**, refer to Chapters 1, 2, and 14.

Picture Puzzle

Tenses in Context. On another piece of paper, write out the following story. Change the pictures and symbols to words. For each of the circled verbs, choose the **simple present**, **future continuous**, or **future perfect continuous**.

This is a letter to Rebecca (the woman in the diving bell earlier in this chapter) from her mother.

A Visit from Rebecca and Leonard

DEAR REBECCA,

WHEN YOU (COME) ↑ ⬜↗ OF YOUR 🌐 ☒ A FEW WEEKS, YOUR FATHER & I (WAIT) FOR YOU ⌂ THE 🚢. BY THAT TIME, WE (LOOK FORWARD) → YOUR VISIT FOR 4 YEARS — EVER SINCE YOU CHOSE THIS STRANGE LINE OF WORK & WENT ↓ THERE.

WHILE WE (WAIT) ABOARD THE 🚢, YOUR BROTHERS & SISTERS (DECORATE) THE 🏠 & (FIX) AN ENORMOUS MEAL (W/OUT ANY 🐟 AT ALL). AS WE (DRIVE) 🏠, THEY (PREPARE) YOUR FAVORITE FOODS, & YOUR NIECES & NEPHEWS (CHASE) EACH OTHER (⬜), (STICK) THEIR 👐S ☒→ THE 🎂, & (PULL) THE 🐕'S TAIL. WHEN WE (ARRIVE) 🏠, THEY ALL (STAND) ⌂ THE FRONT PORCH. AFTER EVERYONE (HUG) & (KISS), WE (CATCH) ↑ 📺 THE NEWS ALL WEEKEND.

WHEN YOU & LEONARD (GET) → THE SURFACE, YOU (HAVE) MEETINGS W/ FAMOUS SCIENTISTS FROM ALL ⌂ THE 🌍, & 📰 REPORTERS (INTERVIEW) YOU BECAUSE YOU (DO) IMPORTANT EXPERIMENTS & (DISCOVER) NEW SPECIES OF 🐟. UNFORTUNATELY, I (DO̶) ANYTHING VERY INTERESTING. I JUST (WASH) 🍽, (BALANCE) THE BUDGET, (TEAR) ⬜↗ COUPONS FROM THE 📰, & (TRY) → FIGURE ⬜↗ HOW → PERSUADE YOU → COME ↑ ⬜↗ OF YOUR 🌐 & STAY W/ US ⌂ DRY LAND.

LOVE,

Mom

Rap It Up

Oral Practice. Work with a partner. Use the calendar below to ask and answer questions about Leonard's and Rebecca's activities in the diving bell. Use the **future continuous** and **future perfect continuous** tenses in your questions and answers.

Examples:
A: What will Leonard be doing in May?
B: He will be gathering fossils.

A: By December how long will he have been taking photographs?
B: He will have been taking photos for six months.

Leonard's and Rebecca's Calendar for Next Year

	Leonard	Rebecca
January	start exploring the ocean	start writing in her journal
February		
March		start laboratory experiments
April	gather fossils	
May		start treasure hunting
June	start taking photos	write reports
July	bake bread	
August		start training dolphins
September	start building a new cell	
October		
November	freeze samples of fish	start preparing for Christmas
December		

Rap in the Real World

Make your own calendar for next year like the one above. Exchange it with your partner and ask each other questions using the **future continuous** and **future perfect continuous** tenses. You may ask questions that bring in information not on the calendar.

FUTURE TENSE REVIEW

Fill in the blanks with the following tenses. In some cases, more than one tense may be possible.

Simple Present (present and future)   **Future Continuous**

Present Continuous (present and future) **Future Perfect**

Simple Future (*will/be going to*)   **Future Perfect Continuous**

A Trip through Time

Tomorrow Norman Norris, the world-famous explorer, (1)_____ (lead) an expedition into the future. This (2)_____ (be) Norman's last expedition because he (3)_____ (retire) next month. By that time, he (4)_____ (explore) not only every corner of the earth in our time, but he (5)_____ (also see) over 25 different centuries.

He (6)_____ (especially look) forward to tomorrow's trip because it (7)_____ (take) him and the other members of the expedition to the year 3000. That (8)_____ (be) the farthest anyone has ever traveled in the time rocket.

Norman and his crew members (9)_____ (work) 12 hours a day right now to prepare for the journey. They (10)_____ (stay) in shape by jogging. They (11)_____ (study) scientific material and (12)_____ (prepare) all of the cameras and equipment. They (13)_____ (take) lots of photographs during their trip. If the photographs (14)_____ (turn out) well, they (15)_____ (be) the first ones ever brought back.

The rocket (16)_____ (leave) at 6:00 tomorrow morning. During the flight, the crew (17)_____ (check) the calendar clock every few minutes to make sure that they (18)_____ (not pass) their destination.

The rocket's first stop (19)_____ (be) the year 2300. While the crew (20)_____ (visit) that time period, they (21)_____ (photograph) the people, animals, and buildings. As they (22)_____ (film) a space station, there (23)_____ (be) an attack from an enemy planet whose people (24)_____ (think) it (25)_____ (be) a military installation. The space station (26)_____ (catch) on fire. As they (27)_____ (watch) the burning station, a woman (28)_____ (scream), "My robot is inside!" Then Norman (29)_____ (run) into the burning station to rescue the robot. The crew (30)_____ (film) as a terrified Norman (31)_____ (run) out with the robot. As the woman (32)_____ (thank) Norman, the robot (33)_____ (spin) around and (34)_____ (bite) Norman on the nose. At that moment, Norman (35)_____ (promise) himself that he (36)_____ (never rescue) another robot for anyone.

During the stop in 2502, Norman (37)_____ (visit) a girlfriend from a previous time expedition. When he (38)_____ (find) her, she (39)_____ (flirt) with another man. Norman (40)_____ (get) very jealous and (41)_____ (start) a fight with the man. The man (42)_____ (punch) Norman in the nose, which by this time (43)_____ (just recover) from the robot bite. Norman (44)_____ (promise) himself that he (45)_____ (never fall) in love again.

After they (46)_____ (arrive) in the year 3000, Norman (47)_____ (conduct) experiments on the environment for several weeks. He (48)_____ (study) the plants and new species of animals that he (49)_____ (find). One day, while he (50)_____ (do) his research, a group of strange people (51)_____ (kidnap) him and (52)_____ (take) him to their village. At first, he (53)_____ (try) to escape. But the villagers (54)_____ (not let) him go. While he (55)_____ (try) to crawl away, they (56)_____ (watch), and they (57)_____ (bring) him back. He (58)_____ (attempt) to escape 35 times when he (59)_____ (meet) the beautiful Zark. In spite of his promise to himself, Norman (60)_____ (fall) in love again. He (61)_____ (not return) to his time. He (62)_____ (live) happily ever after in the thirty-first century with Zark. How (63)_____ (I know) all of this (64)_____ (happen)? My name (65)_____ (be) Zark.

Finish the Story

Use the phrases and pictures on this page to help you rewrite Norman's story. **Do not look back at the original story**. Your story won't be exactly the same as the original, but you should correctly use all of the future tenses and the two present tenses. The verbs on this page are in either picture form or the simple form, but you will choose from the following tenses when you rewrite the story on the next page: **simple future**, **future continuous**, **future perfect**, **future perfect continuous**, **simple present**, and **present continuous**.

Cue Sheet

1. tomorrow lead
   retire next month
   explore

2. look forward
   be farthest

3. work 12 hours a day
   stay in shape
   photographs turn out

4. leave
   check calendar clock
   not pass destination

5. film space station
   catch on fire
   scream
   rescue
   bite
   promise himself never to rescue

6. visit old girlfriend
   flirt
   get jealous
   punch in nose—just recover
   promise himself never to fall in love

7. conduct experiments
   study new species
   kidnap
   take to village

try to escape
try to crawl
bring back

attempt 35 times
fall in love
live happily

A Trip through Time

    The world-famous explorer, Norman Norris, is going to lead an expedition into the
future tomorrow.

Story Line

Use the following Story Line to help you answer the questions on the next page. This Story Line tells you what will happen during Norman and Zark's honeymoon. The verbs on this page are all in the simple form. You should use the correct tense.

Norman and Zark's Honeymoon

Now	Tomorrow	2nd Day
• Read travel books	• Rent a superterrestrial vehicle	• 12:00–4:00—Lie on beach
• Buy new clothes	• 8:00 A.M.—Begin trip	• Norman get too sunburned to sleep
• Study map	• Drive all day	
• Pack suitcase	• 5:00 P.M.—Reach motel at beach	

3rd Day	4th Day	5th Day
• Go diving	• Go to beach	• Norman—Swim
• Norman—Hit nose on ocean floor	• Norman—Lie under beach umbrella all day	• Shark bite Norman's nose
	• Zark—Swim with dolphins	• Zark—Scream

6th Day	7th Day	8th Day
• Norman—Watch super-marine vehicle races	• Norman—Lie under palm tree	• Norman and Zark walk hand in hand on beach
• Bee sting him on nose	• Coconut fall on his nose	• Eat nutrition capsules
		• Take nap in afternoon
		• Go dancing in evening

9th Day
• Go home
• Norman—Schedule nose surgery

Look at the Story Line on the previous page and answer these questions. Use the following tenses: **simple present** (present and future), **present continuous** (present and future), **simple future** (will/be going to), **future continuous**, **future perfect**, and **future perfect continuous**.

1. What are Norman and Zark doing to prepare for their trip?
2. What's the first thing they're going to do tomorrow morning?
3. What time are they leaving tomorrow?
4. How many hours will they have been driving when they arrive at their motel?
5. Why won't Norman be able to sleep on the second night?
6. What's going to happen to Norman when he's diving?
7. Why won't Norman get sunburned on the fourth day?
8. What will Zark be doing while Norman is lying under the beach umbrella?
9. What will Zark do when the shark bites Norman?
10. What will Norman be doing when the bee stings him on the nose?
11. What is Norman going to be doing when the coconut hits him?
12. What are Norman and Zark going to do on the eighth day?
13. What are they eating for lunch that day?
14. What will they be doing that evening?
15. What are they doing on the ninth day?
16. How many times will Norman have hurt his nose by the time he gets home?
17. How many days will they have been honeymooning?
18. What's the first thing Norman's going to do when he gets home?

It's Your Turn. Someone has just told you that you can do or be anything you want. Anything is possible. Tell what you'll do and what your life is going to be like. Use *all* future tenses.

Examples: I'm going to learn to fly a jet.
                   By the time I'm 40, I will have become president.

Fill in the blanks with the following tenses. In some cases, more than one tense may be possible.

Simple Present (present and future)   **Past Perfect Continuous**

Present Continuous (present and future)   **Future in the Past**

Simple Past   **Future** (*will/be going to*)

Past Continuous   **Future Continuous**

Present Perfect   **Future Perfect**

Present Perfect Continuous   **Future Perfect Continuous**

Past Perfect

An Interesting Evening

I.

Dear Mom and Dad,

I am having a wonderful time in this country. There are so many new things to see and do. And the people I (1)_____ (meet) are so interesting and charming that I want to take this opportunity to tell you all about them.

The excitement (2)_____ (begin) on the ship on the way over. There I (3)_____ (meet) my first two friends, Sam and his partner Charlie. They (4)_____ (just return) from exploring the Himalayas. One evening they (5)_____ (tell) me all about their amazing adventure. It seems that in the beginning they (6)_____ (start) hiking on the weekends simply for relaxation. On the first few trips they (7)_____ (make) many mistakes. Of course, at that time, one of them (8)_____ (be) overweight and the other in bad shape. More than once they (9)_____ (think) of quitting. However, they (10)_____ (both be) reluctant to give up. After several months they (11)_____ (become) expert mountain climbers. They soon (12)_____ (become) world famous for climbing even the most difficult mountains. One day a rich businessman (13)_____ (ask) Sam and Charlie to lead a climbing expedition up the Himalayas. He (14)_____ (provide) them with a generous budget and all the able-bodied men they (15)_____ (need) to conduct their expedition. While they (16)_____ (climb), they (17)_____ (have) a lot of problems. Sam almost (18)_____ (fall) off a cliff, and Charlie almost (19)_____ (fall) into a crater. However, they (20)_____ (finally manage) to make

it to the top. Sam and Charlie (21)_____ (tell) me that once
they (22)_____ (reach) the top, they (23)_____ (find)
some rare markings on the rocks. It is unbelievable, but the markings
seemed to be on the walls of the ruins of an old village.

    Sam and Charlie are not the only interesting people I
(24)_____ (meet) since I (25)_____ (leave) home. One night I (26)_____ (attend)
a party given by Frankie, a classmate of mine. I (27)_____ (not know) that Frankie was really
a famous rock star. When Frankie was young, he (28)_____ (want) to be a rock star. He
(29)_____ (think) that he (30)_____ (be) rich and famous. He (31)_____ (dream)
that people (32)_____ (follow) him and (33)_____ (beg) him for autographs. He
(34)_____ (think) that he (35)_____ (spend) his summers lying on a beach on the
Riviera. Frankie is famous now, but he is not happy. He (36)_____ (spend) his days trying to
get away from people with autograph books. His summers (37)_____ (be) so busy that he
(38)_____ (forget) to go to the beach. But Frankie (39)_____ (try) to change his life
again. He (40)_____ (attend) classes at the university and (41)_____ (take) such courses
as algebra, geometry, and calculus. He (42)_____ (plan) to become an engineer. When he
(43)_____ (finish) school, he (44)_____ (move) to a country where they (45)_____
(not know) him and (46)_____ (lead) a quiet life.

II.

    Also at the party there (47)_____ (be) another well-known person, this year's Miss America.
She (48)_____ (be) a gorgeous woman and (49)_____ (be)
everyone's favorite at the party. She was there with a charming foreign
ambassador. Contrary to what you may think, she (50)_____
(not always be) this way. She (51)_____ (say) that at one time
she had been a shy, unhappy young woman. Then she (52)_____
(become) a member of a health club. The owner, Harry, (53)_____
(inspire) her to jog, exercise, and get in shape. She (54)_____
(do) just that since she (55)_____ (meet) Harry. By November
of this year, she (56)_____ (follow) his advice for three years. Nowadays she (57)_____
(not waste) any time. She (58)_____ (get up) every morning and (59)_____ (run) for
five miles, then (60)_____ (swim) 20 laps in the pool. Her schedule (61)_____ (be) strict
for these past few years, but it has been rewarding. Yes, Ellen Wiggley is a very happy person today.

    I (62)_____ (find out) halfway through the evening that the purpose of the party was to
raise money for Laura Kent's presidential campaign. I (63)_____ (see) her posters all over town,
so I (64)_____ (recognize) her as soon as she (65)_____ (walk) in. She (66)_____
(shake) hands with all the guests before she (67)_____ (begin) her speech. If she (68)_____

(win) this election, she (69)_____ (provide) jobs for the needy and food for the hungry. She (70)_____ (say) she (71)_____ (balance) the budget and (72)_____ (improve) the economy. Everyone (73)_____ (applaud) when Ms. Kent (74)_____ (promise): "I (75)_____ (not let) our country be pulled into war. I (76)_____ (not rest) until there is peace on this planet. I (77)_____ (promote) understanding among all people."

III.

She (78)_____ (finish) her speech when suddenly the doors (79)_____ (burst) open and the police (80)_____ (rush) in. The policemen (81)_____ (grab) the man who (82)_____ (flirt) with Ellen. When the commotion (83)_____ (begin), I (84)_____ (talk) to man next to me. We (85)_____ (stop) talking when we (86)_____ (see) the police. Ellen (87)_____ (faint) when the police (88)_____ (arrest) the man beside her. While they (89)_____ (take) him away, one of the policemen (90)_____ (tell) us his story. The man was the internationally known spy Dudley Dangerfield. Dudley (91)_____ (work) as a spy for many years when he was suddenly fired by the only country that (92)_____ (not already fire) him. He (93)_____ (have) one misadventure after another in his career. In recent years he (94)_____ (fill) out one job application after another with no luck. Poor Dangerfield (95)_____ (starve) for months when he (96)_____ (decide) his only choice was a life of crime. The police (97)_____ (catch) him shoplifting several times when they (98)_____ (discover) his true identity.

I (99)_____ (really feel) very sorry for him when the man next to me (100)_____ (tell) me not to worry. He (101)_____ (introduce) himself as Johnny, an employment counselor. He (102)_____ (decide) to become a counselor because he (103)_____ (know) so much about different occupations. He himself (104)_____ (work) at all kinds of different jobs. For example, he (105)_____ (try) to work as a stunt man, then as a roofer. Johnny (106)_____ (say) he (107)_____ (speak) to the police about helping Dangerfield when he (108)_____ (get) out of prison. In addition, if it's possible, Dangerfield (109)_____ (learn) a trade while he (110)_____ (be) in prison. As he (111)_____ (learn) his new line of work, Johnny (112)_____ (counsel) him. By the time he (113)_____ (get) out of prison, he (114)_____ (become) a new man.

Well, Mom and Dad, I (115)_____ (go) on vacation soon. By the time this letter (116)_____ (reach) you, I (117)_____ (live) on a farm in Nebraska for a week. I (118)_____ (go) there with a guy named Elmer, Jr. Ever since I (119)_____ (meet) him, he (120)_____ (tell) me about the wonderful life in Nebraska. By the time we (121)_____ (leave) the city, I (122)_____ (hear) him say at least a hundred times how he (123)_____ (hate) life in the city. I (124)_____ (look forward to) meeting his parents, who (125)_____ (celebrate) their 100th wedding anniversary next Saturday.

Your loving son.

Rap It All Up

Work in a group of four or more people. Pretend you are at Frankie's party. Look at the pictures of the guests below, choose one person, and play the role of that person. Talk to the other guests at the party. Ask them to tell you about what they've done in the past, what they're doing now, and what they plan to do. Learn as much as you can about each guest. These characters can be found throughout this book (chapter numbers follow their names).

Regina (5) Oscar (5) Esmeralda (14) Horace (1)

Shorty (1) Ms. Kent (13) Mr. Talamany (13) Billy (17)

Junior (2) Dudley (10) Lupita (16) Frankie (7)

Ellen (1) Rodney (1) Iona (2)

APPENDIX

Present	Past	Past Participle
arise	arose	arisen
be (am, is, are)	was, were	been
beat	beat	beaten
become	became	become
begin	began	begun
bend	bent	bent
bet	bet	bet
bid	bid	bid
bind	bound	bound
bite	bit	bitten
bleed	bled	bled
blow	blew	blown
break	broke	broken
breed	bred	bred
bring	brought	brought
build	built	built
burst	burst	burst
buy	bought	bought
cast	cast	cast
catch	caught	caught
choose	chose	chosen
cling	clung	clung
come	came	come
cost	cost	cost
creep	crept	crept
cut	cut	cut
deal	dealt	dealt
dig	dug	dug
do	did	done
draw	drew	drawn
dream	dreamed/dreamt	dreamed/dreamt
drink	drank	drunk
drive	drove	driven
eat	ate	eaten
fall	fell	fallen
feed	fed	fed
feel	felt	felt
fight	fought	fought
find	found	found
flee	fled	fled
fly	flew	flown
forbid	forbade/forbad	forbidden

Present	Past	Past Participle
forget	forgot	forgotten
forgive	forgave	forgiven
freeze	froze	frozen
get	got	gotten/got
give	gave	given
go	went	gone
grind	ground	ground
grow	grew	grown
hang	hung/hanged	hung/hanged
have	had	had
hear	heard	heard
hide	hid	hidden/hid
hit	hit	hit
hold	held	held
hurt	hurt	hurt
keep	kept	kept
kneel	knelt	knelt
know	knew	known
lay	laid	laid
lead	led	led
leave	left	left
lend	lent	lent
let	let	let
lie	lay	lain
light	lighted/lit	lighted/lit
lose	lost	lost
make	made	made
mean	meant	meant
meet	met	met
pay	paid	paid
put	put	put
quit	quit	quit
read	read	read
ride	rode	ridden
ring	rang	rung
rise	rose	risen
run	ran	run
say	said	said
see	saw	seen
seek	sought	sought
sell	sold	sold
send	sent	sent
set	set	set
shake	shook	shaken
shed	shed	shed
shine	shone/shined	shone/shined
shoot	shot	shot

Present	Past	Past Participle
shrink	shrank	shrunk
shut	shut	shut
sing	sang	sung
sink	sank	sunk
sit	sat	sat
slay	slew	slain
sleep	slept	slept
slide	slid	slid
slink	slunk	slunk
slit	slit	slit
speak	spoke	spoken
speed	sped	sped
spend	spent	spent
spin	spun	spun
spit	spit	spit
split	split	split
spread	spread	spread
spring	sprang	sprung
stand	stood	stood
steal	stole	stolen
stick	stuck	stuck
sting	stung	stung
stink	stank	stunk
strike	struck	struck/stricken
string	strung	strung
swear	swore	sworn
sweep	swept	swept
swim	swam	swum
swing	swung	swung
take	took	taken
teach	taught	taught
tear	tore	torn
tell	told	told
think	thought	thought
throw	threw	thrown
understand	understood	understood
wake	woke (vi), waked (vt)	woken, waken
wear	wore	worn
weave	wove	woven
wed	wed	wed
weep	wept	wept
wet	wet	wet
win	won	won
wind	wound	wound
withdraw	withdrew	withdrawn
wring	wrung	wrung
write	wrote	written

SPELLING RULES

Present Participles (verbs ending in -ing)

1. For verbs that end in a silent -e, drop the -e before -ing.

   have   ⟶   having   write   ⟶   writing

2. For three-letter verbs with consonant/vowel/consonant, double the consonant before -ing.*

   let   ⟶   letting   tap   ⟶   tapping

3. For four-letter verbs with consonant/consonant/vowel/consonant, double the final consonant.*

   drop   ⟶   dropping   trim   ⟶   trimming

4. For verbs that end in -ie, drop both the *i* and the *e* and add *y* before -ing.

   lie   ⟶   lying   tie   ⟶   tying

5. For two-syllable verbs that end in consonant/vowel/consonant and have the accent on the second syllable, double the last consonant.*

   occur   ⟶   occurring   begin   ⟶   beginning

6. For all other verbs, just add -ing. Don't drop or add anything.

   study   ⟶   studying   beat   ⟶   beating

   deliver   ⟶   delivering   listen   ⟶   listening

Third Person, Singular, Present Tense (adding an -s)

1. For verbs that end in -sh, -ch, -ss, or -x, add an *e* before the -s.

   wish   ⟶   wishes   pass   ⟶   passes

   catch   ⟶   catches   fix   ⟶   fixes

2. For verbs that end in consonant/-y, change the -y to -ies.

   try   ⟶   tries   study   ⟶   studies

3. For all other verbs, just add -s.

   lie   ⟶   lies   drink   ⟶   drinks

The Past Tense or Past Participle of Regular Verbs (ending in *-ed*)

1. For verbs that end in consonant/*-y*, change the *-y* to *-ied*.

    study   ⟶   studied   dry   ⟶   dried

2. For three-letter verbs with consonant/vowel/consonant, double the consonant before *-ed*.*

    tap   ⟶   tapped

3. For four-letter verbs with consonant/consonant/vowel/consonant, double the final consonant before *-ed*.*

    drop   ⟶   dropped   trek   ⟶   trekked

4. For two-syllable verbs that end in consonant/vowel/consonant and have the accent on the second syllable, double the last consonant before *-ed*.*

    occur   ⟶   occurred

5. For verbs that end in *-e*, add just *-d*, not *-ed*.

    translate   ⟶   translated

6. For all other verbs, just add *-ed*.

    want   ⟶   wanted

*Exceptions: Don't double *-x -y*, or *-w*.

     fix   ⟶   fixing

     pay   ⟶   paying

     sew   ⟶   sewing

     pray   ⟶   praying

     draw   ⟶   drawing

Although the following chart is not conclusive, it generally works for cases in this book and can be used as a reference. You will find that it is frequently impossible to use the tenses in Column 3 in *all types* of subordinate clauses. For example, if we take the first item on the chart, we find the following:

I'll help you after you had problems. (impossible)
I'll help you because you had a problem with that. (possible)
I'll help anyone who had a problem on the last exam. (possible)

The use of a certain tense in a subordinate clause is determined by the *type* of clause (adjective clause, adverb clause, clause of time, clause of reason, and so on) as well as by the type of verb.

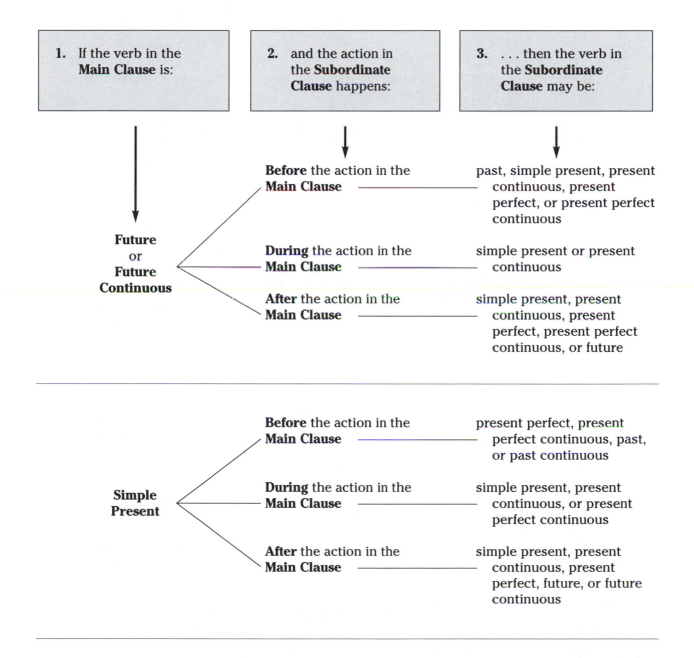

1. If the verb in the **Main Clause** is:	2. and the action in the **Subordinate Clause** happens:	3. . . . then the verb in the **Subordinate Clause** may be:
Future or **Future Continuous**	**Before** the action in the Main Clause	past, simple present, present continuous, present perfect, or present perfect continuous
	During the action in the Main Clause	simple present or present continuous
	After the action in the Main Clause	simple present, present continuous, present perfect, present perfect continuous, or future
Simple Present	**Before** the action in the Main Clause	present perfect, present perfect continuous, past, or past continuous
	During the action in the Main Clause	simple present, present continuous, or present perfect continuous
	After the action in the Main Clause	simple present, present continuous, present perfect, future, or future continuous

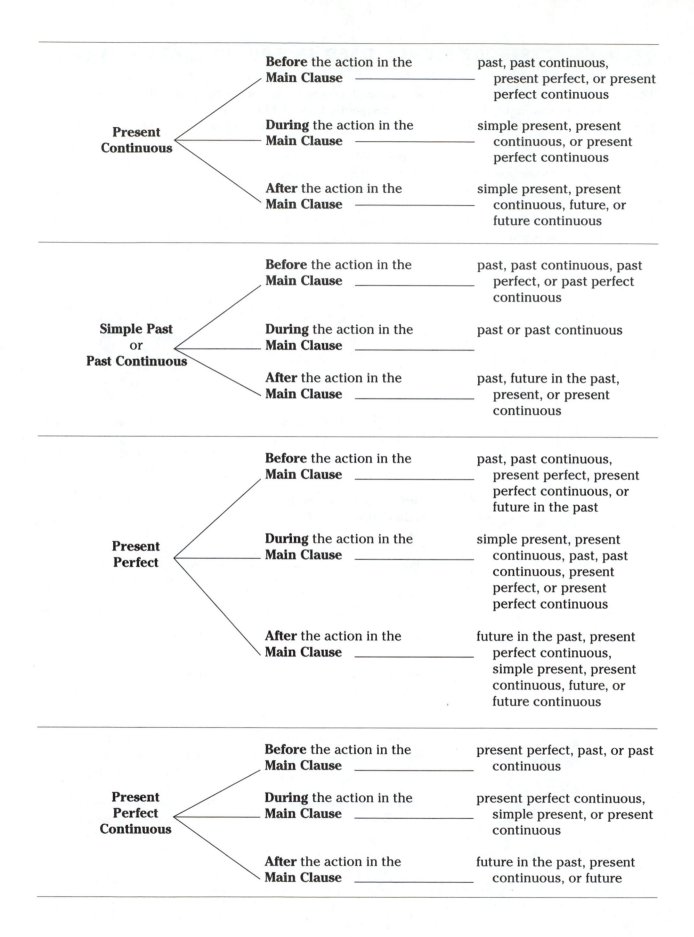

Present Continuous

Before the action in the **Main Clause** ——— past, past continuous, present perfect, or present perfect continuous

During the action in the **Main Clause** ——— simple present, present continuous, or present perfect continuous

After the action in the **Main Clause** ——— simple present, present continuous, future, or future continuous

Simple Past or **Past Continuous**

Before the action in the **Main Clause** ——— past, past continuous, past perfect, or past perfect continuous

During the action in the **Main Clause** ——— past or past continuous

After the action in the **Main Clause** ——— past, future in the past, present, or present continuous

Present Perfect

Before the action in the **Main Clause** ——— past, past continuous, present perfect, present perfect continuous, or future in the past

During the action in the **Main Clause** ——— simple present, present continuous, past, past continuous, present perfect, or present perfect continuous

After the action in the **Main Clause** ——— future in the past, present perfect continuous, simple present, present continuous, future, or future continuous

Present Perfect Continuous

Before the action in the **Main Clause** ——— present perfect, past, or past continuous

During the action in the **Main Clause** ——— present perfect continuous, simple present, or present continuous

After the action in the **Main Clause** ——— future in the past, present continuous, or future

	Before the action in the Main Clause	past, past continuous, past perfect, or past perfect continuous
Past Perfect or **Past Perfect Continuous**	During the action in the Main Clause	past or past continuous
	After the action in the Main Clause	past, past continuous, or future in the past

PASSIVE VOICE

	Active Voice	Passive Voice
Simple Present	He *eats* lunch everyday.	Lunch is *eaten* everyday.
Present Continuous	is eating	is being eaten
Simple Past	ate	was eaten
Past Continuous	was eating	was being eaten
Present Perfect	has eaten	has been eaten
Past Perfect	had eaten	had been eaten
Simple Future	will eat	will be eaten
Future Perfect	will have eaten	will have been eaten

Note: In the passive sentence we use the word "by" with the subject of the active sentence only if it offers important information.

Example: *Active*: The mayor wrote the letter.
Passive: The letter was written by the mayor.

	Direct Speech	**Indirect Speech**
Simple Present	"I eat"	I said (that) I ate
Present Continuous	"I am eating"	I said (that) I was eating
Simple Past	"I ate"	I said (that) I had eaten
Past Continuous	"I was eating"	I said (that) I had been eating
Present Perfect	"I have eaten"	I said (that) I had eaten
Present Perfect Continuous	"I have been eating"	I said (that) I had been eating
Past Perfect	"I had eaten"	I said (that) I had eaten
Past Perfect Continuous	"I had been eating"	I said (that) I had been eating
Simple Future	"I will eat" "I am going to eat"	I said (that) I would eat I said (that) I was going to eat
Future Continuous	"I will be eating"	I said (that) I would be eating
Future Perfect	"I will have eaten"	I said (that) I would have eaten
Future Perfect Continuous	"I will have been eating"	I said (that) I would have been eating

Real/Possible

Future	if + present/present continuous	be going to + simple form will + simple form present continuous

Example: If I remember, I'll call him tomorrow.

Present	if + present	present

Example: If I remember, I usually call him once a week.

Past	if + past	past

Example: If he saw you, why didn't he say hello?
(*It's possible that he actually saw you.*)

Unreal

Future or *Present*	if + past*/past continuous	would/could + simple form

Example: If I had a good memory, I would remember to call.
(*Real situation*: I don't have a good memory, so I don't remember to call.)

Past	if + past perfect (continuous)	would have + past participle could have + past participle

Example: If I had remembered, I would have called him.
(*Real situation*: I didn't remember, so I didn't call him.)

---

*Note: The verb "be" in this case is always "were."

If I were you, I would call more often.

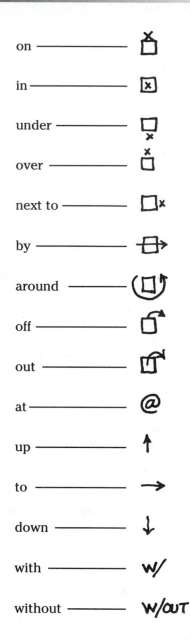

on ——————

in ——————

under ——————

over ——————

next to ——————

by ——————

around ——————

off ——————

out ——————

at ——————

up ——————

to ——————

down ——————

with ——————

without ——————

city ——————

day ——————

home/house ——————

negative ——————

night ——————

sunrise ——————

sunset ——————

morning ——————

evening ——————

expensive ——————

Chapter 1 (Present Continuous/Simple Present)

Figure It Out, page 12:

1. is having (experience)
2. is appearing (perform)
3. guess (suppose)
4. are having (drink)
5. sounds (seem)
6. do/think (have an opinion)
7. smells (have a smell)
8. is seeing (meet with)
9. do/mind (object to)
10. is weighing (put on a scale)

Fill It In, page 13:

1. own
2. sail
3. take
4. sells
5. are arriving
6. are carrying
7. are renting
8. is
9. stands
10. signals
11. is daydreaming
12. is loosening
13. throwing
14. starts
15. prepares / is preparing
16. gives
17. finds
18. drops
19. throw
20. are fishing
21. is telling
22. are eating
23. don't feel / aren't feeling
24. are trying
25. is reeling
26. is taking
27. are helping
28. is also trying
29. always tries / is always trying
30. ends up
31. is forever tripping
32. falling
33. getting
34. are helping (help)
35. is leaning
36. is jumping
37. seems
38. is winning
39. is falling
40. knows

Chapter 2 (Present Perfect/Simple Present)

Picture Puzzle, pages 21–22:

Elmer's brother, Norbert, is 97 and lives alone in the city. He's lived there since he left the farm 75 years ago. He's had an apartment on the top floor of a tall building (high-rise) for the past 20 years.

Norbert is a very charming person, so he has a lot of friends, and he leads a busy life. He almost never gets out of bed before noon (twelve) each morning because he usually stays up late at night. He likes to play cards with his friends in the afternoon. Sometimes he goes to the horse races, and he always wins a lot of money. In the evening he usually takes his girlfriend to an expensive restaurant. He's known her for over 30 years, but he doesn't feel that he's ready to get married.

Norbert knows that many people spend every afternoon in the park, where they sit on a bench and feed the birds. But he's never gone into the park since he came to the city because he thinks that only elderly people go to parks.

Every summer, he takes a train down to his brother's farm and spends some time there. He's there right now. He's only been there for five days, but he's ready to go back to the city.

Norbert and his brother Elmer are very different from each other, and they've argued about everything ever since Norbert arrived on Tuesday. The problem is that Norbert's never liked the life of a farmer. He's complained for four days about getting up at dawn (sunrise) and helping Elmer with the cows. He's fed the chickens and gathered eggs all week, but he hasn't enjoyed it. The truth is that Norbert hates animals. He thinks that horses belong in the races and birds belong in the park, and he's sure that people belong in a city!

Elmer's wife, Iona, has been worried about Norbert's health for many years. She's fed him homemade soup and fresh vegetables all week, and she's made (makes) him go to bed at 9:00 every night. Norbert's worst problem is that she's tried since Tuesday to persuade him to settle down and get married to his girlfriend. He's heard this from her for many years. Every time, he sighs and tells her the same thing: that he's been a bachelor all his life, and he doesn't want to change now.

Chapter 3 (Present Perfect Continuous/Present Continuous)

Fill It In, page 30:

1. has been doing
2. is working
   has been working
3. is always volunteering
   (see page 6, #3)
4. is constantly sweeping
5. cleaning
6. has been doing
7. has been working
8. has been peeling
9. chopping
10. washing
11. is Joey doing
    has Joey been doing
12. is working
13. has been trying
14. are bringing
    have been bringing
15. is using
    has been using
16. is staying up
    has been staying up
17. are only waiting
    have only been waiting
18. is looking
19. is talking
20. is pulling
21. is trying
    has been trying
22. has been trying
23. is always looking
24. has been bribing
25. stealing
26. sawing

Figure It Out, page 31:

1. (number of times)
   Joey has tried to
     escape twice.
   Joey has been trying
     to escape all year.
2. (non-action verb)
   Shorty has owed
     Joey money for
     five months.
3. (specific amount)
   He's lost fifteen pounds.
   He's been losing a lot
     of weight.
4. (frequency adverb)
   Joey's cousin has never
     visited him.
5. (specific amount)
   He has spent $15 on phone
     calls this month.
   He's been spending a lot
     of money on phone
     calls this month.
6. (non-action verb)
   Joey and Shorty have
     known each other
     for three years.
7. (frequency adverb)
   The warden has often caught
     prisoners escaping.
8. (non-action verb)
   He's seemed tired.
9. (number of times)
   They've dug a tunnel
     three times.
10. (specific amount)
    Joey has saved $25
      this month.
    He's been saving some
      money this month.

Chapter 4 (Present Tense Review; page 32):

1. are trying
2. are wiggling
3. screaming
4. chasing
5. is going
   has been going
6. has been waiting on
   has waited on
7. don't fit
   (see page 9)
8. thinks
9. has been having
   has had
   is having
10. has been running
    has run
11. **a**, has been trying on*
    b, has tried on
12. **a**, not putting
    b, not put
13. has been walking
    has walked
14. have been killing
    (This idiom is always used
    with continuous tenses.)
15. walks
16. tries
17. is doing
    does
18. hasn't caught
19. refuses
20. is standing
21. looks
22. sees
23. is walking
24. doesn't see
25. isn't wearing
26. is beginning
27. is tearing
28. has been regretting
    has regretted
29. is

*Note: If you've chosen answer **a** for #11, then the following answer must also be **a**, and so on.

Chapter 5 (Simple Past/Present Perfect)

Picture Puzzle, pages 46–47:

Oscar's wife, Regina, has driven him crazy for years. On their wedding day, they swore to stick together forever, but the romance died soon after the honeymoon.

Oscar has always been rich, but he's never been interested in his money. He's always wanted a simple life. Before he got married, he liked to go camping. He often went hiking up in the mountains. He sat next to a stream in the shade of a big tree or lay in a hammock for hours. On weekends, he liked to stay home and mow the lawn.

However, Oscar's life has been very different since his marriage. Oscar and Regina have gone on four cruises around the world in the past five years. Regina has insisted on Oscar buying her so much jewelry that last April he gave up and bought her a diamond mine. Regina withdrew one-third of the money in their bank account last year, and she has withdrawn another one-third this year.

Recently, the situation has gotten even worse. Last month, Regina tore up the lawn in the backyard and tore down Oscar's hammock. After that, she threw out his favorite fishing pole, hiking boots, and tent.

Oscar has had an ulcer for years. His doctor has often told him to take it easy and to stop smoking and drinking. But Oscar and Regina have just recently found a solution to both Oscar's ulcer and their marriage problems. Last week, Regina agreed to go fishing with Oscar up in the mountains. In return, Oscar agreed to buy Regina a mink tent. They went on their fishing trip and had a great time. They haven't argued about anything since then.

Chapter 6 (Past Continuous/Simple Past)

Fill It In, page 55:

1. happened
2. were having
3. happened
4. was digging
5. was punching
6. was checking
7. matched
   was matching
8. was ordering
9. was repairing
10. were doing
11. began
12. was oiling
13. sounded
14. began
15. stopped
16. were doing
17. were trying
18. was ringing
19. appeared
20. seemed
21. landed
22. held
    were holding
23. watched
    were watching
24. opened
25. stepped
26. hid
27. began
28. began
29. approached
    were approaching
30. reached
31. ran
32. began
33. climbed
    was climbing
34. saw
35. looked

Chapter 7 (Future in the Past/Simple Past)

Picture Puzzle, pages 62–63:

Frankie woke up one day last year and decided that it was going to be (would be) a good day for him. He picked up his guitar and went to his usual place in the park. He put down his guitar case and began to play. He was sure a lot of people were going to come (would come) to listen to him play.

At first, the park was very quiet. There were only a few squirrels and birds who came by because they thought Frankie was going to give (would give) them something to eat. Then a lot of people began to rush by Frankie on their way to work, but he knew they weren't going to put (wouldn't put) any money in his guitar case because they were in a hurry.

Frankie played all morning and thought about his future. He knew that he wasn't going to become (wouldn't become) a famous rock star (singer, musician) in the future. He realized that he was never going to have (would never have) a big house with a swimming pool. He knew that he was never going to be able (would never be able) to buy an expensive car. He was sure that he was never going to travel (would never travel) around the world on a ship. He began to feel really sad.

At about noon (twelve), a policewoman came by. For a minute, Frankie was afraid that she was going to arrest (would arrest) him (or at least chase him out of the park) for playing without a permit. But the policewoman just stopped, sat down on a bench, and listened to him. After a few minutes, she got up, put some money in Frankie's guitar case, and said, "You play very well!"

Then the policewoman told Frankie that she had a brother who worked for a radio station in another city. She said she would talk (was going to talk) with him on the telephone later that day and that she would ask (was going to ask) her brother to have Frankie play his guitar on his radio program.

Well, of course Frankie was thrilled. He began to dream that maybe he really would become (was going to become) a famous rock star (singer, musician). Maybe he would be able (was going to be able) to buy a big house and an expensive car. Maybe he would travel (was going to travel) around the world on a ship. Maybe . . .

Chapter 8 (Recap; pages 64–65):

1. has lived
2. have tried
3. has been
4. decided
5. would build
    were going to build
6. sent
7. would buy
    were going to buy
8. would have to
    was going to have to
9. told
10. wouldn't move
    wasn't going to move
11. began
12. sent

13. got
14. found
15. was sitting
16. were wondering
17. appeared
18. chased
19. were screaming
20. running
21. arrived
22. took
23. started
24. hid
    was hiding
25. made
    was making
26. clung
    was clinging

27. growled
    was growling
28. sat
29. asked
30. was happening
31. appeared
32. became
33. were
34. decided
35. wouldn't build
    weren't going to build
36. was
37. threw
38. has been
39. have noticed
40. has become

Chapter 9 (Past Perfect/Simple Past)

Fill It In, pages 76–77:

1. went
2. had never been
3. were
4. had gone
5. had been
6. looked (see page 161)
7. had slept
8. had looked
9. were
10. had been
11. ate
12. slept
13. fought
14. played
15. had done
16. drove
17. stuck
18. gave
19. told
20. was
21. were
22. came
23. drove
24. had never seen
25. didn't get
   (= didn't have an
      opportunity)
26. had dived
27. was
28. had forgotten
29. was
30. had fed
31. had been (at Lion Country
      Safari)
   was (in general)

Chapter 10 (Past Perfect Continuous/Past Continuous/Simple Past)

Picture Puzzle, pages 84–85:

Dudley Dangerfield had been looking forward to his vacation for a long time when he finally got to Hawaii. He had been working very hard and needed to relax. On his first day at the hotel, he laid his towel on the beach and lay down on it. He put on his sunglasses and began to read a book on flying. While he was reading, he fell asleep. When he woke up, he realized that he had been sleeping for three hours, and his first day was almost over.

On his second day, he was lying in a hammock under a palm tree when he started to think about his health. He was a little overweight because he had been eating a lot of terrific international food ever since he had gotten his first job as a spy. He decided to go on a diet, sweat in the sauna every day, and jog five miles every morning. He was thinking (had been thinking) about getting in shape for the Annual International Spy Tennis Tournament when suddenly he heard a loud scream from somewhere down the beach.

He jumped up and ran down the beach to see what the commotion was. He saw a woman in the water. She was screaming and thrashing around and appeared to be drowning. On the beach, a few people were running around and trying to find a lifeguard. Dudley jumped in, swam out, and pulled her to shore. Someone on the beach spread a towel on the sand, and Dudley put her on it. Someone else in the crowd said that the woman had been trying to swim to shore from a yacht. Finally, the woman opened her eyes, and Dudley saw that she was fine. He also noticed that she was gorgeous. He was beginning to fall in love with her when the police ran up and arrested her. They said that she was an international criminal who had been following Dudley for several weeks. She had been planning to kidnap him for her government since the first of the month. The police had been trying to capture her since she had gotten to Hawaii.

That evening, while the sun was slowly setting, Dudley took a walk up the beach. As he was walking (walked), he thought with regret about his would-be romance. He considered exploring a new line of work.

Chapter 11 (Past Tense Review; pages 86–87):

1. began
2. was
3. hadn't ever gone
   had never gone
4. hadn't been eating
   hadn't eaten
5. joined
6. was
7. had been worrying
   had worried
8. ran
9. swam
10. took
11. sweated
12. thought
13. was sweating
    sweated
14. dreamed/dreamt
    was dreaming
15. had told
    ("at that time" =
    before that time)
16. was changing
17. thinking

18. came
19. told
20. had just begun
21. was
22. said
23. told
24. had mentioned
25. went
26. walked
27. was giving
28. was pointing
    pointed
29. had put
30. sank
31. saw
32. said
33. had been coming
34. teaching
    had taught
35. told
36. had weighed
37. started
38. was
39. swore

40. was
41. was eating
    ate
42. thought
    was thinking
43. had changed
    was changing
44. had become
    was becoming
45. hadn't eaten
46. had been exercising
    had exercised
47. had been thinking
    had thought
48. had tried
49. was drinking
    drank
50. remembered
51. had recently left
52. had become
    was becoming
53. had preferred
    preferred
54. had traded in

Chapter 12 (Cumulative Review); pages 92–94:

I.
1. was
2. got
3. stuck
4. set
5. sold
6. learned
7. have loved
8. worked
   was working
9. wasn't
10. were forever going
    (see page 53, #6)
11. began
12. had already shut
13. was sitting
14. had already eaten
15. were growing
    had grown
16. thought
17. was going to throw
    would throw
18. were
19. began
20. led

21. looked
22. traveled
23. had been seeing
    ("see" = find)
    had seen
24. had been warning
    had warned
25. had been threatening
    had threatened
    was threatening
26. gave
27. watched
28. went
    was going
29. were doing
30. was getting
31. had been
32. was doing
33. were trying
34. yelled
    was yelling
35. had already climbed
36. had just stepped
    were just stepping

II.
37. happened
38. had caught
39. sneezed
40. lost
41. crashed
42. looked
43. lost
44. caught
45. fell
    was falling
46. hung
47. was sweating
48. saw
49. had collapsed
50. had fallen
51. held
    was holding
52. clung
53. let
54. was
55. was going to faint
    would faint
56. knew

57. would probably break
    was probably going
       to break
58. fell
59. slid
60. landed
61. was
62. fled
63. had just squeezed
64. were now trying
65. ran
66. split
67. was trying
68. headed
69. was running
70. was wondering
71. would happen
    was going to happen
72. sprang

73. fled
74. hid
75. was
76. chose
77. was forever happening
    (see page 53, #6)

III. 78. began
79. ended
80. waited on
81. went
82. have worked
    have been working
83. graduated
84. is
    has been
85. sit
86. have
87. answer

88. give
89. comes
90. asks
91. stole
92. have tried
93. happens
94. am sitting
95. hoping
96. am thinking
97. am beginning
    have begun
98. have worn
99. have answered
100. haven't done
101. isn't
102. have seen
     have been seeing
103. have already decided

Chapter 13 (Simple Future: Will/Be Going To)

Figure It Out, page 103:

1. promise/no
2. prediction/yes
3. prediction/yes
4. promise or volunteered action/no
5. plan/no
6. promise or volunteered action/no
7. plan/no
8. determination/yes
9. prediction/yes
10. plan/no

Fill It In, pages 104–105:

1. will be
   is going to be ⎫
2. will be   ⎬ prediction
   is going to be ⎭
3. will fire (promise)
   is going to fire (plan)
4. hire
5. will fix (promise)
   are going to fix (plan or prediction)
6. will serve (promise)
   are going to serve (plan)
7. will have (promise)
8. will cut
9. will have (promise)
   is going to have (plan)
10. will work (prediction)
    is going to work (plan or prediction)
11. will give (prediction)
    is going to give (plan or prediction)
12. is going to promise (plan)

13. will make (promise)
    is going to make (plan)
14. is going to provide (plan)
15. is going to stop ⎫
16. is going to buy ⎬ plan
17. is going to work ⎭
18. is going to draw
19. glue
20. will say (prediction)
    are going to say (plan)
21. will cut out (promise or determination)
22. will be able (promise)
    are going to be able (plan)
23. will have to (promise or determination)
    are going to have to (plan)
24. will find (determination)
25. will be
    is going to be
26. is going to give (plan)
27. will be

Chapter 14 (Simple Present [meaning the future]/Simple Future: Will/Be Going To)

Picture Puzzle, pages 111–112:

Esmeralda sees that she'll have (she's going to have) problems with money in the future if she doesn't change her way of doing business. She'll have (She's going to have) three main problems.

First, people will begin (are going to begin) to drive by her little shop on their way to big shopping centers. They won't see (aren't going to see) her sign in the window in their hurry to get to a big store.

Another problem will be (is going to be) her eyesight. As she gets older, her eyesight will get (is going to get) worse. In the future, it'll be (it's going to be) difficult for her to see images in her crystal ball.

But Esmeralda's worst problem will be (is going to be) that people will stop (are going to stop) believing in gypsies with crystal balls because they'll think (they're going to think) that crystal balls are out of style. When they do that, they'll stop going (they're going to stop going) to fortune tellers, and Esmeralda's business will be (is going to be) in terrible trouble. Young people won't beg (aren't going to beg) her for advice on romance anymore. Rock stars won't offer (aren't going to offer) her money and jewelry for advice on music. Detectives won't ask (aren't going to ask) her for help in catching criminals.

As soon as Esmeralda makes some big changes in her business, she'll stop (she's going to stop) worrying, and she won't have any more trouble with ulcers. But because she'll always be (she's always going to be) a stubborn, independent woman, she'll refuse (she's going to refuse) to make any changes until the city government decides to evict her and tear down her house (shop). When they do that, she'll have to (she's going to have to) move her business to a shopping center. After she moves, she'll get (she's going to get) some glasses and buy advertising in all the local newspapers. Then she'll throw (she's going to throw) out her crystal ball and buy a computer.

As soon as a customer sees her computer, he'll know (he's going to know) that Esmeralda is a very modern fortune teller. Soon, thousands of people will begin (are going to begin) to come to her new shop. She'll hire (She's going to hire) more people and open branch offices. Every office will have (is going to have) a computer. In a few years, she'll have (she's going to have) a whole chain of offices, and business will be (is going to be) terrific!

Chapter 15 (Present Continuous [meaning the future]/Simple Future: Will/Be Going To)

Fill It In, page 121:

1. will really like
    are really going to like
2. will be
    is going to be
3. will do
    are going to do
    are doing
4. will have to
    are going to have to
5. are loading
6. will count
    (volunteered action)
7. are loading
8. will watch
    (volunteered action)
9. will get
    are going to get
10. are doing
11. will get
    (volunteered action)
12. will finish
    are going to finish
13. will read
14. are driving
15. will unload
    are going to unload
16. will ring
17. will hold
18. are carrying
19. are spreading
20. will listen
21. will watch
22. are rolling (see page 159)
23. will tell (promise)
24. will be
25. are finishing
26. will go
27. will hand
28. are hammering
29. will clean up
    are going to clean up
30. will tell
31. will be
    is going to be
32. are you going to go
    are you going (plan)
33. will be
    am going to be
    (prediction)
34. won't get
    aren't going to get

Chapter 16 (Future Continuous/Simple Future: Will/Be Going To/Present Continuous [meaning the future])

Picture Puzzle, pages 128–129:

My parents are bringing (are going to bring/will be bringing) my new baby brother home from the hospital tomorrow morning and life will be (is going to be) just terrible for me. My parents won't pay (aren't going to pay) any attention to me anymore. While my mother is feeding him, I'll be doing my homework without any help. While I'm reading my school books out loud, my father won't be listening because he'll be playing with my baby brother. While I'm swinging in the backyard, my brother will be crawling across the lawn, so my parents won't be watching me. As my brother is growing up, I'll be shrinking into the background.

However, I have a plan. At midnight (twelve) tomorrow night, I'll be hiding (I'll hide/I'm going to hide) under my brother's crib, and I'll wait (I'm going to wait) until my parents are sleeping. Then I'll grab (I'm going to grab/I'm grabbing) my brother and quietly creep (creeping*) out of the house. I'll get (I'm going to get/I'm getting) on a bus and take (taking*) him back to the hospital. I'll trade (I'm going to trade/I'm trading) him in on something else: maybe a dog or a horse or a robot.

On the other hand, maybe I won't steal him. If I do, the police will probably arrest (are probably going to arrest) me for kidnapping. My mother will probably faint (is probably going to faint), and my father will yell (is going to yell) a lot and tear out his hair. No, I won't trade him in. Instead, I'll teach (I'm going to teach) him things. For example, I'll teach him to play Hide and Seek. While I'm hiding, he'll be looking for me. And I'll teach him to ride a bicycle (bike) and build a toy house and float in the pool. I'll teach him about the animals in the zoo, too. Of course, while he's learning all these things, my parents will be ignoring me. I'll be teaching him all day long, but my parents will probably think (are probably going to think) he's a genius.

I know what I'll do (I'm going to do). I'll run (I'm going to run) away from home! One night, when my parents are sleeping, I'll pack (I'm going to pack/I'm packing) my suitcase (bag) and quietly creep (creeping*) out of the house. I'll get (I'm going to get/I'm getting) on a bus and leave (leaving*) the city far behind. While my little brother is growing up, he'll wish (he's going to wish/he'll be wishing) he had a big sister to teach him about bicycles (bikes) and pools and animals and parents!

*Note: With compound verbs, the two actions should be in the same form, but the auxiliary verbs are omitted from the second action.

Chapter 17 (Future Perfect/Simple Future: Will/Be Going To/Simple Present [meaning the future])

Fill It In, page 135:

1. will have run
2. will have stuck
3. will have fallen
4. rings
5. will have lost
6. will have torn
7. will finally come
   is finally going to come
8. will be
   is going to be
9. will have heard
10. won't have understood
11. will have explained
12. arrives

13. will get
    is going to get
14. will take
    is going to take
15. recover
16. will have failed
17. fail
18. will promise
    are going to promise
19. rolls around
20. will be
    is going to be
21. will have complained
22. will have gotten

23. will be
    is going to be
24. will sit
    is going to sit
25. sweat
26. return
27. will have forgotten
28. will take
    is going to take
29. will have considered
30. will have sworn
31. begins
32. will be
    is going to be

Chapter 18 (Future Perfect Continuous/Future Continuous/Simple Present [meaning the future])

Picture Puzzle, page 142:

Dear Rebecca,

When you come up out of your diving bell in a few weeks, your father and I'll be waiting for you on the ship. By that time, we will have been looking forward to your visit for four years—ever since you chose this strange line of work and went down there.

While we wait aboard the ship, your brothers and sisters will be decorating the house and fixing an enormous meal (without any fish at all). As we drive home, they'll be preparing your favorite foods, and your nieces and nephews will be chasing each other around, sticking their hands into the cake, and pulling the dog's tail. When we arrive home, they all will be standing on the front porch. After everyone hugs and kisses, we'll be catching up on the news all weekend.

When you and Leonard get to the surface, you'll be having meetings with famous scientists from all over the world, and newspaper reporters will be interviewing you because you will have been doing important experiments and discovering new species of fish. Unfortunately, I won't have been doing anything very interesting. I will just have been washing dishes, balancing the budget, tearing out coupons from the newspaper, and trying to figure out how to persuade you to come up out of your diving bell and stay with us on dry land!

Love,

Mom

Chapter 19 (Future Tense Review; pages 144–145):

1. is going to lead
    is leading
2. will be
    is going to be
3. is going to retire
    will be retiring
    is retiring
4. will have explored
5. will also have seen
6. is especially looking
7. will take
    is going to take
    is taking
8. will be
9. are working
10. are staying
11. are studying
12. preparing
13. will be taking
    will take
    are going to take
14. turn out
15. will be
    are going to be
16. is going to leave
    is leaving
    leaves

17. will check
    is going to check
    will be checking
18. don't pass
    (see page 159)
19. will be
    is going to be
    is
20. is visiting
    visits
21. will be photographing
    will photograph
    are going to photograph
22. are filming
    film
23. will be
    is going to be
24. will think
    are going to think
25. is (see page 159)
26. will catch
    is going to catch
27. watch
    are watching
28. will scream
    is going to scream
29. will run
    is going to run

30. will be filming
31. runs
32. is thanking
33. will spin
    is going to spin
34. bite
35. will promise
    is going to promise
36. will never rescue
37. is going to visit
    is visiting
38. finds
39. will be flirting
40. will get
    is going to get
41. start
42. will punch
    is going to punch
43. will have just recovered
44. will promise
    is going to promise
45. will never fall
46. arrive
47. will be conducting
    will conduct
    is going to conduct
48. is going to study
    will be studying

49. finds (see page 159)
50. is doing
51. will kidnap
    is going to kidnap
52. take
53. will try
    is going to try
54. won't let
    aren't going to let

55. is trying
    tries
56. will be watching
57. will bring
    are going to bring
58. will have attempted
59. meets
60. will fall
    is going to fall

61. won't return
    isn't going to return
62. will live
    is going to live
65. is
63. do I know
64. will happen
    is going to happen

Chapter 20 (Cumulative Review; pages 150–153):

I. 1. am meeting
       have met
       have been meeting
    2. began
    3. met
    4. had just returned
    5. told
    6. started
       had started
    7. made
       had made
    8. was
       had been
    9. thought
       had thought
    10. were both
        both were
        had both been
    11. became
        had become
    12. became
    13. asked
    14. provided
    15. needed
    16. were climbing
    17. had
    18. fell
    19. fell
    20. finally managed
    21. told
    22. reached
        had reached
    23. found (see page 161)
    24. have met
    25. left
    26. attended
    27. didn't know
        hadn't known
    28. wanted
    29. thought

    30. would be
        was going to be
    31. dreamed
    32. would follow
        were going to follow
    33. beg
    34. thought
    35. would spend
        was going to spend
    36. spends
    37. are
    38. forgets
    39. is trying
    40. is attending
    41. taking
    42. is planning
        plans
    43. finishes
    44. will move
        is going to move
        is moving
    45. don't know
        (see page 159)
    46. lead
II. 47. was
    48. is (in general)
        was (at the party)
    49. was
    50. hasn't always been
        hadn't always been
        wasn't always
    51. said
    52. became
    53. inspired
    54. has been doing
        had done
    55. met
    56. will have followed
        will have been
          following

    57. isn't wasting
        doesn't waste
    58. gets up
    59. runs
    60. swims
    61. has been
    62. found out
    63. had seen
        had been seeing
    64. recognized
    65. walked
    66. shook
    67. began
    68. wins
    69. will provide
        is going to provide
    70. said
    71. would balance
        (promise)
    72. improve
    73. applauded
    74. promised
    75. won't let
    76. won't rest
    77. will promote
III. 78. was finishing
        had finished
    79. burst
    80. rushed
    81. grabbed
    82. was flirting
        had been flirting
    83. began
    84. had been talking
        was talking
    85. stopped
    86. saw
    87. fainted
    88. arrested
    89. were taking

90. told
91. had been working
92. hadn't already fired
93. had had
94. had filled
    had been filling
95. had been starving
96. decided
97. had caught
98. discovered
99. was really feeling
100. told
101. introduced
102. had decided
103. knew
104. had worked
    had been working
105. had tried
106. said
107. would speak (promise/volunteered
    action)
    was going to speak (plan)
108. got (indirect speech)
109. will learn
    is going to learn
110. is

111. learns
    is learning
112. will be counseling
    will counsel
    is going to be counseling
113. gets
114. will have become
115. am going to go
    am going
116. reaches
117. will have been living
    will have lived
118. am going
    am going to go
119. met
120. has told
    has been telling
121. leave
122. will have heard
123. hates
124. am looking forward to
125. are celebrating
    will be celebrating
    will celebrate
    are going to celebrate

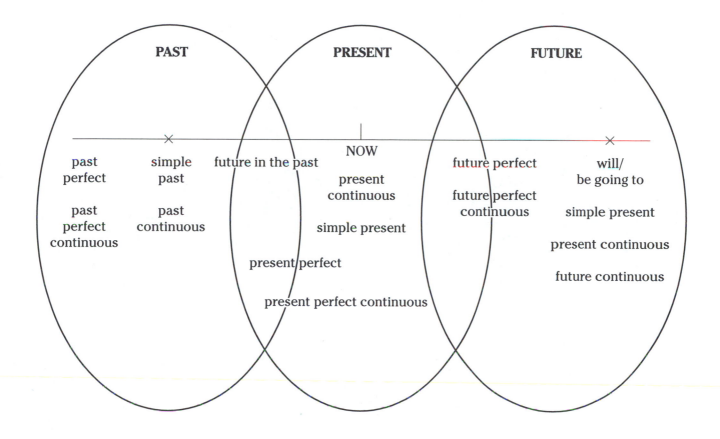

NOTES

NOTES

NOTES